LAUGHTER
─AND─
TEARS

6/492

LAUGHTER
—AND—
TEARS

Forty-Eight Addresses for Baptisms, Weddings and Funerals, with Preface

Frank Pagden

MONARCH
CROWBOROUGH

First published 1995

ISBN 1 85424 300 4

British Library Cataloguing-in-Publication Data.
A catalogue record for this book is available
from the British Library.

Designed and Produced in England for
MONARCH PUBLICATIONS
Broadway House, The Broadway, Crowborough,
East Sussex TN6 1HQ by
Nuprint Ltd, Harpenden, Herts AL5 4SE.

The funeral talks are dedicated to all those families
who allowed me to share their grief,
and the baptism and wedding addresses
are dedicated to my wife,
without whom I wouldn't have known
what I was talking about.

Other books by Frank Pagden:
Looking Sideways at God (SPCK)
The Man Who Chopped History in Half (Epworth)
The Gospel According to St Lynas (Monarch)

CONTENTS

INTRODUCTION

Personally, I blame the choir. When I arrived, they gleefully told me of a previous minister who had just three wedding addresses. In the vestry, beforehand, they used to speculate on which one he'd use, and knew them so well that they could have prompted him had he stumbled. It was a rotten trick to tell me this because, as they well knew, it put me on my mettle to think up a new address every time they were at a wedding.

To these I have added addresses for baptisms and funerals which have been the product of much midnight meditation over recent years, and might be a source of ideas for others. The least I can do is share what I consider the best of them with my colleagues in the ministry, to whom I owe so much. There is no other book of this kind available in this country to my knowledge, and hopefully, this volume will fill that gap on the study shelf.

Clearly, these talks are personal to me, and cannot be preached by anyone else as they are, but they may provide some ideas and insights, quotes and stories, and save time. As you will see, they had varying applications; to the committed Christian, the uncommitted, the second marriage, the suicide, the child death, etc. The inevitable personal touches can easily be adapted, the personal stories put in the third person or substituted, and extra biblical material can be added as desired at suitable points without interrupting the flow.

Frank Pagden

WHAT SHALL WE SAY AND HOW SHALL WE SAY IT?

As the baptism and wedding guests stream into the church for their great day most will be looking around in curious wonder. The last time many of them met was at grandma's funeral, and that may not have been in a place of worship, so this could be the first time some of them have *ever* been inside a church at all, let alone this one.

If they come to a crematorium funeral, it could be, for younger people at least, a first experience with any kind of religious atmosphere.

For them the set-up is completely strange and the service a novelty, so they will be nervously anticipating being required to do embarrassing and unusual things (like saying the Lord's Prayer when they don't know it, or standing when they should sit or kneel). They don't know how to behave in such surroundings and are afraid of committing a procedural gaffe. In the pew leaflets of our church which we place round at weddings, we have been forced to add a paragraph pointing out that, although laughter and applause are acceptable at suitable points, smoking and drinking in the pews and taking flash photographs every fifteen seconds, just aren't done. At the crematorium, clear instructions need to be given at every point.

Some guests are also uneasy about being 'got at' by whoever is conducting the service. They've seen too many caricatures of 'hot-gospellers' browbeating their congregations to death, weird religious oddballs frightening them to death, or wimpish clergy boring them to death, to feel comfortable about what they are about to undergo.

Yet they come, hopefully and with open minds, and (except at funerals) cheerfully — willing to let the Church share in their family occasion. Most feel that the Christian church isn't elbowing into their lives, sticking a foot in the door, nor do they feel that it is acting in a merely official or bureaucratic way: rather, most welcome the church's role for what it can add to their family experience on such an important day.

What a missionary opportunity! By the starboard stirrup of John Wesley's horse (I write as a Methodist), what preacher worth the name could resist such an chance! Here is an opening to show the Jesus-pilgrimage as attractive, challenging, and more life abundant; to demonstrate that deep religious meanings are at the heart of our relationships; and to emphasize that man does not live by supermarkets alone. To avoid saying anything at such times would be a dereliction of duty. After all, we are commanded by scripture to preach the Gospel on only two occasions — '*in season, and out of season*' — and baptisms, weddings and funerals are definitely '*in season*'.

Although this opportunity to address the unchurched stranger ought to be grasped firmly, it must also be handled with sensitivity and care, unless by too much enthusiasm or lazy blundering we nullify or neglect the message in our charge.

Of course, the total impact of the whole service is the important thing. The words, the music, the actions, the atmosphere, will combine to create an overall impression. This should be two-fold.

First, there must be a sense of the transcendent, the holiness, the timelessness of God. Without that, we might as well be officiating at an up-market Register Office. So the celebrant should not be afraid of suitable pauses and silences (as long as they are designed and don't make anyone feel uncomfortable because no-one knows what should happen next). They enable those present to soak up this ambience. It helps, too, to take the most significant parts of the service with great solemnity and with deliberation, allowing each word to 'register'.

The other note which should be struck is one of easy friendliness — of the Church as a welcoming spiritual home. It helps to have a few words of explanation with the visitors before the service starts to welcome them, to introduce the organist, the verger, and the choir, and explain what will happen in the service, the sound loop system and any other 'nuts and bolts'. If there's one thing about the event that is certain, it is that no-one will remember a single word of the address. So it is my practice to give the bride and groom at a wedding, the parents at a baptism (and sometimes the relatives at a funeral) a printed copy of it afterwards.

These two elements can fight together, yet both have somehow to be combined within the same act of worship. All transcendence and no friendliness can make the service cold and distant, all friendliness and no transcendence and we might as well be a social club. The art is to control and balance the divine and human in such a way that neither destroys the other, and to move gently from one to the other, using music (a hymn, perhaps) as a transition.

Turning to the address, there are some guidelines which I have found useful. Communication was once defined as trying to carry a heavy parcel of an idea across a chasm to someone on the other side. The task at the beginning, and indeed continuously thoughout, is to build bridges, before one can even start across with the burden.

So the search is on to find common ground with the hearers upon which to build that bridge. It can be a shared experience, a shared sense of humour, a shared prejudice, a common memory — anything which makes the listener give a little mental nod of agreement. It's not important how religious or secular those start points are, it's where one finishes up that matters. As the congregation comprises a great variety of people, that bridge must either be a very wide one, or there must be several going in different directions. Until those bridges are built, it's pointless even starting to convey the central idea.

Jesus, of course, was a great master at this. When he was with shepherds he talked about sheep, when with farmers, about crops; as far as we can tell in the gospels he always used the familiar substance of people's lives upon which to base his message.

So, bridges built, one lifts up the central idea to carry it across. But what idea? Is it applicable? Is it something the people across the chasm want or can use? For example, it would be folly to preach about the dangers of riches to a congregation who are all on social security, to talk about The Lord's Day to those who haven't a Lord, or to rely on the authority of Holy Scripture in speaking to people who don't think it's holy or has any authority for them. It would be equally unwise to feed the hard meat of the Gospel to those, like most family guests, who could only digest the milk of The Word in small doses.

On the graduated scale of spiritual development people move by stages from Atheist, through Agnostic, Questioner, and Seeker to Convert. Only God knows what is really going on in people's minds, but it's a fair assumption that in the average service on such an occasion the whole range will be represented. The role of the preacher is to move people one stage up the scale. The temptation is to treat everyone as if they were seekers, ready to be challenged to commitment. But it would be unrealistic to expect one sermon or address to move people more than one stage in the process. By trying to move people too fast and too far one can do more harm than good. Even that great preacher, John Wesley, claimed that, through his preaching, people were only 'awakened'. The mysteriously divine process of conversion happened, and still happens, mostly in private, in one-to-one counselling, or small intimate groups.

So the idea must make contact with the congregation

where they are, apply to their real situation, be within their spiritual and mental 'reach', and carry them one step nearer to where you would like them them to be. In the case of most guests this is what is called PRE-evangelism; the creation of an image and atmosphere.

With the baptism and Church membership addresses, I have intentionally avoided any theology of what baptism is. For some, it symbolizes in good biblical fashion the death of self and the new life in Christ. For others, particularly with infant baptisms, the main theme is the equally biblical prevenient Grace of God. Yet others, who prefer adult baptisms, see its main theme as commitment and dedication, which is just as Bible-based. Rather than take sides in this, I felt that the addresses would be more useful if such issues were left out, to be added by others if they felt so inclined.

Someone said regarding funerals that, 'at the grave side we are all universalists!' I reckon that is true. Condemnation at such times is out of place, judgement is God's prerogative, not ours. In any case, the mourners at a funeral are too aware of their hurt, too wrapped up in their loss, to pay much attention to any high-flown doctrines. A funeral is no place for close-reasoned, theological argument, however admirable. Such addresses usually serve as little more than a verbal anaesthetic, and end up conveying very little. I take issue with giving such addresses, however, and feel that surely there must be a way to communicate something useful and helpful at such times. Even if the close family is too numb to listen, one has to remember the other people are present, and say something to make them think about the eternal realities.

Unfortunately for preachers who prefer an easy life, the use of overly-explicit religious language is a 'turn-off' for most people these days. For instance, terms like 'salvation by faith' are totally incomprehensible to the ordinary man in the street. Though we may be very used to this sort of language, he is not, so such language though not, naturally, the thought contained therein, must be avoided whenever possible.

Too much jolliness, and what can appear to be handling

holy things with over-familiarity and flippancy, also create negative reactions in people. The address can have its light-heartedness and laughter, but it must also have its tears. The humour must be securely based on a deeply serious conviction, and the preacher's conduct must be sincere and personal.

The use of humour in preaching is a wonderful thing, because it preserves a sense of proportion and judgement. Care has to be taken with it, of course, and it must only be used when it is fitting and appropriate. I find that, like any jewel, a funny illustration must be put in a setting. It must be 'flagged' so that the listeners know to expect something to laugh at, and it must illustrate what it is supposed to highlight. Some speakers can use it better than others — happy those who can! I have found that even at funerals humour can sometimes play its part, when one is sure of one's ground. For instance, I have occasionally been able to say something like: 'I know it may be a bit flippant, but I can't help wondering whether St Peter had a problem with some of the unruly young angels, and decided that the only thing to do was to send for Kathleen. I can just see her sorting them out, can't you?'

Lastly, the high art for preachers is in combining the simple and the profound, so that listeners can receive the message at many different levels, depending on their level of spiritual development. Any idiot can be simple, and any clergyman can be profound, but it takes dedicated hard work by the preacher to try to be both at the same time. We see this facility supremely at work in Jesus's parables, of course. The perfect illustration is that wonderful text that lies at the heart of the whole of Christian belief and behaviour, and which runs like a golden thread through all the addresses in this book, yet is amazingly compressed into three one syllable words: 'God is Love.'

For those of us who normally speak only to insiders, preaching to outsiders is a demanding matter. The easier it looks the harder it is, for the art conceals the art. The first art is in doing it effectively, and the second art is making it look easy.

But remembering our Lord's great commission (and with a sideways look at the starboard stirrup of John Wesley's horse), we recognize it as our duty. We tackle our task, God help us, as faithfully and joyfully as we can, in his name and with his strength.

I

INFANT BAPTISM

AS CHILDREN SEE US

A young lad walked into the lingerie section of a department store and asked to buy a slip for his mother's birthday the following day. But when it came to what size to buy, he was at a complete loss. 'Well, what's your mother like?' asked the assistant. 'Is she thin or fat, tall or short?' 'Oh, she's just perfect,' said the lad. So the shop assistant sold him a size 14. The next day a rather large lady came in and swapped it for a size 24. Well, that was how he saw her.

There's the story of a father who was standing by his little boy's open bedroom door. The little lad said his prayers as he was taught, but added: 'Dear God, make me a great big good man like Daddy.' That's how he saw his father. The father went into his bedroom and prayed, 'Lord make me a great big good man like my boy thinks I am.'

When as parents and grandparents we catch the children looking at us, it makes us wonder what they're thinking. Just how do they see us?

I remember when our children were small and we were off camping, I had to run to catch a bit of paper which was blowing away. 'Daddy *ran*,' they said, 'He *ran*!'. It was the talk among the children for days. Now whether they thought

I was so decrepit that I'd fall apart above five miles an hour, or whether I'd been telling them so often to stop running and walk sensibly that they thought I was theologically against it, I don't know. But it was how they saw me, definitely a 'non-runner'!

So consider these babies today. As they grow up among us and in their family circles, they'll be watching us with hawk eyes, marking everything, making mental notes of us, and copying us as much as they can. You'll be watching them as parents and relatives pretty closely, but believe me, they'll be watching you with even more care. So it's a worthwhile and sobering question to ask ourselves this morning — what will they see? How will they see us as they grow up? I've a few suggestions to make. There are three qualities which are implicit in the Christian faith that I would want my grandchildren to see in me, and I hope you would want your children to see in you.

1. HARMONY

There are people who are permanently at war within themselves. Most of us, at some periods of our lives, have inner conflicts which threaten to tear us apart. Sometimes it's the conflict between what we know we ought to do and what we feel we want to do. Sometimes it's between what our bodies want and what our minds decide. It's at times like that when we realize what a blessing it is to have an inner poise and harmony, to have that balance, and be at peace with oneself. That's what the Bible means by *holy*; whole, wholesome, complete, in harmony within ourselves, with our neighbours and with God.

The founder of the Iona Community, George McLeod, once said, 'We have become too holy in the "holy, holy," sense, whereas we should be biblically holy — that means facing up the totality of life.'

You don't have to read the Gospels for long before you see that Jesus was typically Jewish in his view of mankind. He didn't divide us into soul and body, but regarded us as whole people. And, as Christians, we take this view of human beings. A good and healthy balance between spiritual, mental and physical is important for us, and for those around us.

It's this, or the absence of it, that the children will see in us as they grow up. It's this wholeness that they'll try to imitate — they'll see it as an ideal which they'll want to aim for themselves. If we can achieve it, it'll remain in their minds' eyes for the rest of their days. I pray that with God's help, we'll succeed in that.

2. INTEGRITY

When a baby is born to us a new person steps into our belief-system, whatever it is. The standards we have, they will absorb quite automatically. They may reject them for a while in their rebellious teenage years, but they'll always have them there in the back of their minds.

So we must stand for what we believe in, for their sake as well as ours. After all, if you don't stand for something — you'll fall for anything. And it's this central core of what we *are* that is the crunch point, isn't it?

For instance, you have the opportunity to take something which isn't yours, and no-one will ever know who took it. What do you do? That's when integrity shows itself.

You are put in a position where you can satisfy yourself but only at the cost of hurting someone else in the process. What do you do? That's when you know whether you have any integrity or not.

You are in a position of power over people you dislike, you can spread rumours about them, demote them, denigrate them, and in general make their lives more difficult. What do you do? Have you any integrity?

This sort of integrity cannot be bought or sold, inherited, rented or imported — it's home grown. It's you and me, stripped down to essentials.

And our children are going to see that — see us as we

really are, integrity or not, honest or not — make no mistake about that. We can't pull the wool over their eyes.

And it's not only what we *don't* do that is our integrity, but what really gets us going. It has been said that you can measure a person's integrity and greatness of character by what makes them angry, and what makes them laugh. Compare the anger of a little man who gets upset with trifling things, with the anger of the likes of William Booth of the Salvation Army who shouted:

> While women weep as they do now, I'll fight; while little children go hungry as they do now, I'll fight; while men go to prison, in and out, in and out, I'll fight; while there is a poor lost girl upon the street, I'll fight; while there yet remains one dark soul without the light of God, I'll fight, I'll fight to the very end.

That is the anger of integrity. Would that there was more of it today!

What we stand for, what we laugh at, what we are angry at, what moves us, what disappoints us, what we're willing to sacrifice for — all this will rub off on these children today. We must make it a noble stand worth imitating, we must hand on to them values that will not let them down as they test these values for themselves.

3. THE STRENGTH OF OUR LOVE

There's a great argument going on these days about renewable energy resources. The Welsh are getting uppety about windmills dotted over their hills, people are still designing new wave machines, hydroelectric schemes are being suggested — the Severn Barrage, and all that. But there is one renewable resource which would warm our hearts rather than our feet, it's love.

That great Catholic theologian Teilhard De Chardin wrote:

Some day, after mastering the winds, the waves, the tides and gravity, we shall harness for God the energies of love, And then for the second time in the history of the world, mankind will discover fire.

Obviously he means, and I mean, Christian love, not the romantic love of Mills & Boon, or the Hollywood musicals. Real, robust, practical, Christian love:

> The love which has the hands to help other people,
> The love which has the feet to go about doing good,
> The love which has the eyes to see misery and need,
> The love which has the ears to hear the cry of the
>   starving and the refugee,

That's what Christian love looks like. If you want a fuller version, read the story of Jesus in the Gospels.

That sort of quality, worked out in the joys and sadnesses of family life, in its challenges and its opportunities, its changes and development, that's what will rub off on the children brought up within that family. They'll see quality life as it should be lived, and they'll measure their future relationships by it.

May we show them by how we live what real unselfish, sacrificial family love is like.

Deitrich Bonhoeffer, that great German theologian murdered by Hitler, once said:

> The family is a Kingdom of its own within the world, a haven of refuge amidst the turmoil of our age. It's not founded on the shifting sands of private and public life, but has a peace in God. It is an ordinance God has established in the world, the place where peace, quietness, joy, love, respect, tradition, and, to crown them all, happiness may dwell.

And I would add, where Wholeness, Integrity and Love may be seen and imitated.

2

INFANT BAPTISM

POTENTIALS

Reading: John 3:1-8

Isn't it infuriating when you half remember something and can't track it down. I've spent all week trying to remember who said, 'Of what use is a baby?' It was some famous scientist, who was showing someone his great discovery. I've got the feeling that it was Rutherford at Cambridge, who first split the atom. When he described the process and the result to someone, they said, 'Of what use is that?' So Rutherford (if it was him) replied, 'Of what use is a baby?' Quite.

Today we've entertained and been entertained by five of them. Little dictators, all of them. The house is thrown sideways, all the carefully laid plans the parents make go out of the window, the timetable revolves around feeding times, nappy times and bath times, and proud mother and father ring up proud grandparents to say, 'You'll never guess — he's just done his first burp!' When the first one arrives, we say, 'However did we waste our time before the baby came?' When the second one arrives we say, 'What a wonderful restful time we had when we only had one,' and so it goes on.

Yet, think of it from the baby's point of view. Sitting in

24

wet nappies, either hungry or full of wind, can't read, can't talk, can't understand what's going on. What an existence!

I don't know what your youngest memory is. The earliest one I've heard of is from Tolstoy who recalled what it was like to be a baby:

> I am all bound up; I want to stretch out my arms and I cannot, I scream and cry and I hate my own screaming. But I cannot stop. People are leaning over me — I can't remember who, and everything is shrouded in semi darkness. There are two of them. My screaming affects them; they are anxious; but they do not release me as I want them to, and I scream still louder.

A lot of ladies love babies, they go all maternal, and they say they'd like babies to stay babies. But I don't think they really would. Too demanding, too wearing.

1. The important thing about babies is not what they are but what they'll become. It's their potential that makes babies more than just living dolls for broody females.

Every mother and father has crept into the nursery in the quiet night hours, looked at their sleeping baby, and wondered, 'What's he going to be when he grows up? What sort of person will he grow to be? What job will he do? Who will he marry? What joys and sorrows, what pride or shame, what laughter and tears will he bring us?'

Potential, that's the important thing about babies.

2. Potential is what they bring to our families as well. Instead of being just a couple living your relationship, and in general pleasing yourselves, suddenly there's someone else to worry about, someone totally dependent on you, at your complete mercy. You've stopped being just a couple and you're now a family.

Now that changes your priorities and your reactions.

The BBC Audience Research Department says that it's when the baby comes that listening habits change. Up to then people listen to wall-to-wall pop; wallpaper music. But this sudden load of responsibility means that the couple start listening much more to speech-based programmes. They need information and advice.

Then you begin to see that your family has a potential, the probability of advancing into the next generation. This, your child, will go further into the future than you will. Your genes, of course, will be carried on, but so will be your attitudes, your values, your standards — ferried by your children into a world you can only guess at. Now that's a sobering thought!

What are the attitudes, the values and the standards, that our children will inherit from us? Are they worth passing on? Are they going to help our children be the fine upstanding generation we want them to be, or will they let them down at times of stress?

When babies come into the house we make sure the water is safe for them to drink, the air is as pure as we can make it, we check the food we give them, the bed-clothes we cover them with, and we make sure the cat can't get in the cot.

Perhaps we ought to examine more carefully the mental and spiritual diet we give to the children; to be more concerned about giving them good values, noble standards, examples of unselfish and warm loving, generous judgements, and a strong sense of family loyalty and togetherness.

The coming of a baby gives our ordinary families great potential. They can become great universities of life, where we all learn to love.

3. The other potential I want to mention is our own spiritual latent capacity. This is the factor which in the Church we call being 'born again'.

The term has been brought into disrepute because of religious extremists of various kinds. Their judgemental unkindness does them no credit. One television evangelist said, believe it or not, that Mother Theresa wouldn't go to heaven because she wasn't born again.

I did hear a story about one Welsh seaman, a member of a very strict sect, who was dumped on a south sea island when the crew couldn't stand him any longer. Five years later he was discovered by another ship, and they found to their amazement that he'd built himself two chapels. One he went to every Sunday for his devotions, so they asked him what the other one was for. 'That,' he said, drawing himself up to his full height, 'is the one I *don't* go to!' But why should we let such people hijack a perfectly good religious truth?

It started, as you remember, from our reading. Nicodemus, a respected religious leader of many years standing, comes to Jesus by night so as not to be seen. He sees in Jesus much that he admires. He is told, 'You must be born again — born from above.' The words carry both meanings.

'How can a man be born again from above when he is old?' replies Nicodemus. He is a church leader, has inherited a great tradition of spirituality as a pharisee, he's tested it in the experience of life, he's conformed his life to it, measured his habits, his conduct, his speech, even his thoughts and feelings by it. How can he break away from all this and start again?

Jesus replies, 'You must first be born of water, go and repent in the Jordan with John the Baptist, then be born in the spirit, come and join my disciples and follow me.'

Did he? There's a tradition that this timid man was baptised after the resurrection by Peter and John, was deprived of his status by the Jews and banished from Jerusalem.

But the point is that his challenge is everyone's challenge. Jesus asked him, and by proxy asks us to, 'wake up to a new life.' He throws open the windows to a new world, and says, 'Look at this new dimension. Explore, launch out, be born again.'

There are turning points in all our lives. Times when circumstances make us change — marriage, illness, unemployment, retirement, bereavement, the coming of a baby. At such times it's human nature to start to search. For help, for encouragement, for inspiration — as Nicodemus did.

It's at those times that we get a glimpse of what life is really all about. It's at those times that Jesus challenges us.

Start again, he says — think of the potential. Many times in our lives he says that to us. But this time start from a deeper spiritual basis, build on the ultimate realities that you've just discovered lie deep inside you. Start from the truths you've just realized in what Jesus tells you. Construct your life anew on the love and joy and peace that He shows you. Be born again from above.

With the coming of your baby, you are compelled to start afresh. Make that new start at a higher level than before, at God's level.

Today we have gathered here, I know, an enormous range of personal experience — birth, bereavement, retirement, illness. Between us there's hardly a facet of human life that we don't represent.

We bring it all before God, lay the weight of it down, and ask God to bless it and us — that's what worship is.

In return, God gives us the strength and resources to start again, to be born again, to take our strength from on high, and to go from here living on a higher level, with a glint in our eye, and a spring in our step.

That's the Gospel — that, indeed, is the Good News.

3

INFANT BAPTISM

BRINGING UP BABY

Y ou have brought your babies here today for baptism, as thousands have before you. It's a happy day, proud parents, delighted grandparents, fond uncles and aunts, have all gathered round for what is an important occasion for your family. This child is firmly rooted in your home circle, and today is to play its part in your belief system.

For you've decided that you want your children to grow up as Christians, not as Moslems, not as Jews, not as Atheists, but within a Christian atmosphere and against a Christian background.

You do this, because, as good parents, you want to provide the best you know for your children.

You can't bring up children in a test-tube, you can't surround them with cotton wool and protect them against outside influences. You can't bring them up neutral. Life just isn't like that.

You will, when they start developing teeth, be teaching them to clean their teeth. Teeth are a problem, aren't they. They hurt when they're coming, they hurt when they're going, and you've only got to clean them when you've got them. But you'll be encouraging your children to use a toothbrush, you'll be insisting, you'll even be bullying them to clean their teeth.

You don't say, 'Well, we'll leave it until they're grown up. Then they can decide whether they want to clean their teeth or not.' Of course, you don't say that — when they leave home they'll clean their teeth or not, regardless of what you say. But in the meantime, as good parents, you'll get them to clean their teeth. You'll hope it becomes a good habit — because it's the best thing you know to do with them.

The same principle applies to moral questions. All children are little uncivilized heathens really until you teach them otherwise. As your children grow up you'll be teaching them to share their toys with other children. You'll be teaching them what belongs to them and what belongs to others, and that taking someone else's things is stealing, and a thing you get punished for.

You'll be telling them how to tell the truth, and that not telling the truth is lying, and a serious breach of personal relationships. As the next few years pass you'll be trying, like all good parents, to instill basic moral standards into them.

You don't say, 'Well, we won't bother about all that. Let them decide when they're adult whether they want to be selfish or unselfish people, honest or dishonest — truthful or untruthful people.'

You don't do that. When they leave home they'll become what they'll become regardless of what you say — but in the meantime, you, as good parents, will be hammering home the virtues of being unselfish, honest and truthful, hoping that it'll become a good habit. Why? Because it is the best you know — and you want the best for your children.

Today you have brought your children to be included in the Christian family, to be brought up against a Christian background. You can't bring them up as moral and spiritual neutrals, so you are doing this on their behalf, because, as good parents, you are providing for them the best you know. When they leave home they'll hold on to what you've taught them, or they won't. They'll go their own way. But a lot of it will stick, and remain in their minds all their lives.

The big questions they'll ask as they grow up, are the big ones all adults face:

1. Where did I come from?
2. Why am I here?
3. What am I supposed to do while I'm here?
4. Where am I going?

Now the Christian religion gives answers to these questions which are at the heart of the meaning of life. And they are answers which have given a satisfying purpose to life for people over the last 2000 years. They aren't easy answers, they can be grappled with on many levels. But answers they are.

Christians should know:

where they've come from;
why they are here;
the broad principles of how they should act while they
   are here; and where they're going.

For Christians, these big questions have been answered, and we can get on with the business of living.

There's a lot of concern these days about children brought up without proper moral training. We're always reading about the spate of crime by children. That, and the business of the murder by two children in Liverpool stirred the nation to ask itself, 'What sort of standards, or lack of them, are we giving our children these days?' Indeed! What sort of training are they getting, in the home, the school and the Church? Are they ever taught the difference between right and wrong?

You, as new parents, have a difficult job — more difficult these days than a generation ago. With all the pressures and dangers surrounding your children, you have to some- how teach them the difference between good and bad so strongly that they'll be able to resist the pressures of the school playground, and the group persuasion of their peers. I'm convinced that there is no stronger shield than a good Christian belief system.

1. Teach them to believe in a God who cares, and by whom they're loved and accepted. Children can feel very vulnerable, miserable and rejected. Tell them that the Creator who made them loves them, whatever they've done, and however they feel. Then they'll never be worthless in their own eyes. Their self-esteem, though it'll take some knocks, as we all have to accept, will never be completely gone, because they'll have God's price ticket on them.

If they can live comfortably with themselves and have their own integrity, their own convictions, they'll be able to live comfortably and constructively with others.

2. Teach them about Jesus, the man who lived a 'pro-active' life of self-giving, and who provided a window into what God is like. Tell them Jesus' stories, about the Good Samaritan, the Sower and the Seed, the Prodigal Son, the lost sheep, and all the others. They're good stories, ideal for children, and they all underline the quality of life Jesus led, and which God wants us to live.

Behind me, on the wall of the church are the Ten Commandments — lots of older churches have them displayed. Nothing wrong with them as a moral standard, but they're the basics. They're nearly all 'Do Nots'. That's bottom gear. Jesus shifts us into top gear, his teaching isn't do not, but do. It's positive, it's 'Go and *do* likewise.'

If we want our children to grow up to be resolute, life-affirming people, who are part of the world's healing and not its hurt, there is no better training than a Christian one to do that.

Teach them — *show them* — that there's a dimension of religious experience all around them. From the stones of an ancient cathedral, to the beauty of a wonderful view. Get them to feel the exhilaration of Handel's Messiah, and the miracle of a new-born kitten. Introduce them to a world full of mystery and wonder, of miracles and love.

One of the most valuable things you can do for them is to get them to experience a dimension that is beyond sight and touch, but still very real.

That's God's patch, and where we can feel him close. Children are usually better at this than we hard-boiled adults are. Maybe, in the process, we'll learn more from them than they will from us.

My son once rang us up from London. He said he'd had a mind-blowing experience the previous week, 'I suddenly looked at myself and said "I'm walking through a Garden Centre, with my wife beside me, and the baby in a buggy — by heavens — I'm domesticated!"'

Well, so are you. Somehow, with God's help, you've got to make good as parents. And it isn't easy, for there's one thing children wear out quicker than shoes — it's parents.

A woman got on a bus with seven children. The bus driver asked her, 'Are they all yours, or is it a picnic?' 'They are all mine,' she replied, 'and believe me, it's no picnic!'

Well, one, two, three or seven, it's still no picnic. Your children will bring you great joy, and perhaps sorrow, laughter and tears. Certainly they'll bring the enormous challenge to become good parents.

We here, at the Church, will continue to try to help, and pray for you.

May God who made the family as the most important unit in society, bless you and your children in the years ahead.

4

INFANT BAPTISM

THE FAMILY SCHOOL

I heard of a young mother who gave birth to twins, and rang the local newspaper to put a notice in the personal column. She gave the girl at the other end all the details, but unfortunately it was a crackly line, and the newspaper girl asked, 'Will you repeat that?' 'Not if I can help it,' was the reply.

How often I wonder, after a hectic day with the children, do we look at them and say just that. And yet...

Once a humble Methodist minister, scraping away on a very low salary, must have thought that, when he was often discouraged by trying to bring up his three lively daughters. In later years he was mightily cheered, when one ended up as the wife of a famous artist, another married a man who was later to be Prime Minister, and the third became the mother of Rudyard Kipling.

Yes, parenthood is often tough, but how many people can look back on loving Christian parents, and supportive homes, where they could be truly themselves, without pretence, and still be loved and valued.

How many people can look back and find that in their childhood there was laid a sure foundation of character and personality, and the good aspects of what they are now?

Yes, what a father and mother say to a child may not be heard outside the door of their house, but it will reverberate in history. It will be echoed in the adult life of their children, and, in turn, will be passed on to their children.

1. THE FAMILY IS A SCHOOL FOR LIFE

All children, however lovable, are at bottom little barbarians. They have to learn at home, in gradual easy ways, or in hard ways, all sorts of lessons, such as:

> how to share;
> how to treat other people considerately;
> how to do what they're told by people who know what's what;
> how to absorb, consciously or unconsciously, the self-discipline that makes achievement possible;
> how to discover that one can win long term goals by giving up short-term pleasures.

All these things, and many others, they learn by example, by teaching, or by compulsion, in any good family. The family is a school for life skills, for learning how to live tolerantly and successfully in community.

All this takes time, parent time, for it can't be skimped. I heard of a couple who went into a toy shop. 'We both work,' she said, 'so the kids are left alone a great deal — what have you got for them?' The shop assistant suggested one thing after another, but nothing seemed to suit. 'You don't seem to have much idea!' said the mother. 'Well Madam,' replied the shop assistant, 'as far as I see it, what your children need most is a mother and father, but we don't sell them here.'

Family time is priority time. So put it high on your list, even in these hectic days when meals are thawed out rather than thought out.

2. THE FAMILY IS A SCHOOL FOR LOVE

It's the place where we learn that love isn't a matter of liking. We choose our friends, we don't choose our relatives, or our children — we're stuck with them. With luck we may like them, but we have to learn to love them, and they have to learn to love us.

They will learn to work for each other's good. They'll get into the habit of thinking of others before themselves. They'll know what it feels like to be open, vulnerable, and self-giving. They'll experience trust, confession, forgiveness, — all those deep human emotions that lie in and around the word *love*. They'll discover within the security of your family, all that battery of things that are involved when you unpack that most profound of human attitudes.

Of course, love is defined many different ways. Mills & Boon define it one way in their romantic novels, the old Hollywood musicals define it another way, but here, in church, we define it in the most demanding and rewarding way of all — we use the Christian definition. And for that we look at the four Gospels, Matthew, Mark, Luke and John. We see the picture of Jesus, what he was, what he did, and we say, 'Yes, that's the best definition of love we have ever seen.'

It's tender, yet very strong. It not only includes joy and laughter but also suffering and tears. The greater the love, the greater the price-tag there is on it. The more you love someone, the more you care about them, the more you worry about them, the more you are concerned for them, the greater is the hurt when something happens to them. The greatest love of all, the love Christ had for us all, involved the greatest price-tag — a cross.

Professor Barclay told a moving story of a mother whose son was killed in the First World War. 'O that I might see him again,' she prayed. Well, the story goes that an angel, moved by her grief, appeared to her and said, 'Yes, I'll arrange it — but how would you like to see him, as a proud soldier in the front line or as the little baby he once was?' 'No', said the mother, slowly, 'I'd like to see him as he was one day when he'd been naughty out in the garden, and he ran in to ask my forgiveness. He was so small and unhappy, and the tears ran down his grubby face, and he flew into my arms so fast he knocked the breath out of me.'

There is nothing more moving than someone in a loving relationship who says, 'I need you.'

Your children need you to teach them the joy of a love like that — the heart warming power of giving sacrificially — the cost and the positive rewards of forgiving generously.

3. YOUR FAMILY IS A SCHOOL FOR THE WIDER COMMUNITY

Like everything else, the family at its best is a small microcosm of the larger family of God. Having learned the basics in our individual families we can then go on to take our place in the wider family of the Church and the yet larger family of humankind.

Exercising the skills, and qualities we have learned at home, we can venture out and demonstrate compassion, sympathy and understanding, and make our own contribution to the intractable problems out there.

We can take our place in the adult world, standing four-square on our integrity and convictions, knowing that we see ourselves properly, as God sees us, neither as arrogantly proud or hypocritically humble, but as loved sinners.

Like everything else God made, the existence of the family is not an accidental phenomenon. It's not just a sociologically convenient way of propagating the species. The family says something more. It speaks of a deeper level of experience, a larger purpose in his providence, and the ultimate destiny that God has in store for us.

The family, *our* families, are small models, here and now, where, through happiness and sorrow, successes and disappointments, we learn the depths of character that will fit us for God's larger family in his eternal kingdom.

So, as parents, you have a tremendous responsibility.

I'm sure that as you look at your baby when it's asleep in the cot, you're suddenly aware, as all parents are, of the responsibility you carry. And it *is* a great and difficult task — I wouldn't try to tell you otherwise. But there's nothing more useful and satisfying than bringing up a family well. You're the headmaster and headmistress of your own private little school; teach your children well. For your future happiness, and theirs depend on it.

I finish with the story of that old preacher, Gypsy Smith. A lady once wrote to him and said, 'I feel led to going around preaching as you do; the trouble is that I have nine children and can't see how I'd ever manage to get away to fulfil that call.' Gypsy Smith wrote back. 'My dear Madam, I am delighted to hear that the Lord has called you to preach; I am also pleased to note that he has already provided you with a ready-made congregation.'

Start where you are, in the demanding ground of your home, and never cease promoting healthy, happy and holy family life, until that basis is soundly laid in your home, in our community, and in our world. And may God bless you as you do it.

5

INFANT BAPTISM

GOOD RELIGION

Reading: Acts 5:27-39

There's good politics and bad politics. There are political systems, like democracy, with all its faults, which does at least serve the good of most of the people most of the time. There are bad political systems, which lead people to civil war, bankruptcy, starvation and disaster. What we can't have is no politics because human beings are bonded into communities, and those societies have to have some sort of framework, some kind of organization — and that's politics. So you can have good politics or bad politics; what you can't have is no politics. It's not possible.

There's good religion and bad religion. There are religions which, with all their faults, do serve the spiritual aspirations of people — which express and feed the deepest feelings and the highest aspirations we have. They preach and practise goodwill to humanity, and foster understanding, sympathy and compassion.

There are other religions which take people's genuine sincere searchings and lead them to disaster. The dreadful events which sometimes happen in cults and fanatical fundamentalist sects, mass murder, and suicide, as well as emotional manipulation and thought control, show just how evil a bad religion can be. What you can't have is *no* religion. Because deep down everyone has religious feelings, thoughts and instincts. It's how we're made. We may reject an orthodox religion, but all we are doing is transferring that loyalty and faith, that religious motivation, to something else. To our own mind, our own self-interest, or some other secular god.

So the problem we have is to sort out the good religion from the bad religion. It's an important decision, because we do it, not just for ourselves, but, as we remember today, for our children too. In the case of the babies brought here today, you in the family are very careful, quite rightly, about the purity of what they eat and drink, the safety of their cots and buggies. You keep an eye on them nearly all the time, watching over their well-being. On a deeper level, you have to be just as sure that the religion in which you bring them up is a good and healthy one and not a bad and destructive one. How can we tell the difference? What tape-measure can we use to tell if a religion is true and good, or false and bad? We don't want to judge by hearsay, or prejudice, or be swayed by eloquent speeches, or fashionable ideas. What impartial measurement can we use?

That was precisely the problem the first Christian preachers presented to the Jewish government way back in the early days. The Jewish leaders had to decide whether this new movement was good or bad, constructive or destructive. Should they help it or try to destroy it? You heard the story in our Bible reading for today. And they heard, and we heard, the wise advice of Gamaliel. He was a pharisee himself, but was far more than that. He was not only respected, but loved. People called him, 'the beauty of the Law.' He was one of the few men to whom the title Rabban was given, (an extra-special Rabbi) and when he died they said, 'Since Rabban Gamaliel died, there has been no more reverence for the law, purity and abstinence has died out.'

So Gamaliel pondered the problem, and in his wisdom warned the Jews, 'Don't act against these men, if what they do is of men it will come to nothing, if it is of God you cannot stop them.' What he was saying was that time will sort the good from the bad. The falling leaves of the calendar will make it all plain. If this religion is evil, it will destroy itself, and you will see the ruin of it. If the theology is wrong, it will show itself to be ridiculous, without any effort on our part. However attractive it is, if it doesn't work in human life and experience, if it doesn't help in a crisis, doesn't comfort in distress, doesn't provide a channel for joy and a work site for peace, it will fall of its own weight. We don't need to push it over.

There were many such religious movements in his day, as there are now. Plenty of sects and cults. They flourished for a time, then died; either they slowly withered, or ended in a bloody confrontation. And he quoted two examples that his listeners knew about.

One of them was led by a man named Theudas, who made big claims for himself, claimed to be able to divide the waters of Jordan with his command. He, and many of his followers ended up dead in a battle with the Romans.

The other example was Judas of Galilee. Quirinius was appointed governor of Palestine in AD 6, took a census and started taxing the Jews. Judas of Galilee led an insurrection which claimed that as God was the true ruler of the Jews they should pay their tax only to him, not the Romans. The Romans crushed it, but the remnant lived on as the Zealot movement.

So as Gamaliel said, time is the best measure of what is good religion and what is bad. Time is not only the best healer, but the best judge.

We stand today in the main stream of a Christianity that has stood the test of nearly 2000 years. Ours, like all mainstream churches, does not claim any doctrines or beliefs that differ in any major way from the faith of all of our sister churches. We stand and say the creeds, and when we do that we proclaim our oneness with the other Christians across the world and down the years.

Time has battered the Church throughout the centuries. It has been oppressed, persecuted, ignored and subverted at various times to selfish and political purposes. In short, almost everything that could have happened to the Christian Church in the last 2000 years *has* happened. Everything time could have thrown at the Church has been thrown. And still it stands.

John Wesley, who founded the Methodist movement 250 years ago was always writing pamphlets, and one of them was 'The Principles of a Methodist.' It could stand as the attitude of any Christian in any mainstream church. In one paragraph he says this:

Religion we conceive to be no other than love. The love of God and of all mankind; the loving God with all our heart and soul and strength, and the loving every soul which God hath made, every person on earth as our own soul.

This love we believe to be the medicine of life, the never failing remedy for all the evils of a disordered world, for all the miseries and vices of men. Wherever this is, there are virtue and happiness going hand in hand. There is humbleness of mind, gentleness, longsuffering, the whole image of God, and, at the same time, a peace that passeth all understanding, and a joy unspeakable and full of glory.

This religion we long to see established in the world, a religion of love and joy and peace; having its seat in the heart, in the inmost soul, but ever showing itself by its fruits; continually springing forth, in every kind of beneficence, spreading virtue and happiness all around it.

This is the heart of Christianity as he saw it, and that has lasted for 2000 years. The message of self-giving love which we see in the life and message of Jesus has inspired and challenged the minds of all centuries. The warmth and strength of his presence has given courage to faint hearts, and comfort to lonely souls for millennia.

History is littered with the husks of cults who have flourished and died, the books are full of stories of movements who could not stand the dread hand of time — who could not adapt, who could not respond to the deep down needs of the human spirit. Who, when faced by Gamaliel's stern test, failed.

But today we receive these children into our own belief system, into a Christianity which has survived all these centuries. Into a Church which is human, and because it is human, has within it the seeds of its own decay. But it is also Godly, and because of that, it has within it the seeds of its own renewal. And that constant renewal and reformation as the centuries pass, means that the heart of the Christian faith — that love of God and mankind, which Wesley described, is re-presented in new forms to each century as it comes.

These children will, God willing, be living in the 2070's, when we'll all have joined the majority. I don't know whether one of the main industries then will be ICI, probably not. Will they still be eating Kelloggs? Will Marks and Spencers still be at our street corners? Most interesting of all, will MacDonalds be running the British government? Probably not. After all, not many of our well known names were about 100 years ago, how many will survive another hundred? Very few I guess, and in 500 years, none.

But of one thing I *am* sure. The religion in which we have received these children today will still be here. The buildings might be different, the worship will be different, and the organization will be different, but the central message we preach today — the proclamation of God's love, and our response, will still be preached. They, their children and their grandchildren, will receive the message of a good religion that has lasted and will last — because as Gamaliel pointed out, it has within it the things of God.

6
ADULT BAPTISM/CHURCH MEMBERSHIP
FISHERS OF MEN

You and I are now the successors of those first men who heard Jesus saying, 'follow me'. We're in a great long line of men and women who for the last 2000 years have heard his voice and responded to him, as Peter, James, John, Andrew, and the others did. They were fishermen, and he called them to be fishers of men. And that's interesting.

1. OUR PREDECESSORS WERE VERY ORDINARY PEOPLE

They weren't unemployed or on their beam ends.
They were ordinary busy working people.
They were average folk.

At the end of Jesus' life, the authorities asked, 'Have any of the rulers or the pharisees believed in him?' Apart from one or two, whom we know about, the answer was 'no'.

These four pioneers came directly from ordinary life, ordinary work, ordinary families, and ordinary homes.

They couldn't have been more human.
They had petty ambitions between themselves.
They quarrelled.
They weren't outstandingly brave, because at the cru-
cifixion they ran away.
They weren't a quartet of clones, but four individuals.
By all accounts, Peter was headstrong and impulsive.
Andrew was homespun and loyal.
James and John were 'sons of thunder,' whatever that
meant.

They were representative. We could find four people
just like that up our main street any day of the week, and in
our church any Sunday.

So when you think of that great line of Christians, into
whose inheritance you now come, don't think of them as
somehow super-human — they weren't. Don't think that
they were anything other than ordinary human beings, just
like you and me.

But they had heard Jesus' voice saying, 'follow me,' and
seen his beckoning finger. And, like you, they got up and
did so.

2. THEY SERVED GOD WITH WHAT THEY HAD

St Augustine once said that fisherman Peter didn't lay aside
his nets, he changed them. He still used his fisherman's
skills, even though the lake had changed. He still had to be
patient with people, as patient as he was when waiting for
the fish to come. He still had to persevere, all night if necessary, in order to make his witness. He did it for fish, it was
the least he could do for people.

He needed his courage to face turbulent crowds — the
courage of a fisherman who prayed because his boat was so
small, and the sea so rough.

He had to have an eye for the right moment to say what
he had to say, just as a fisherman must time his work. He
still had to fit the bait to the fish he was aiming at. And oh,

there were so many things in the fisherman's trade that he took with him into his discipleship.

Yes, he didn't give up his nets — he changed them.

As you leave school, go on to further education, and into your chosen careers, don't think that to be a Christian is somehow to decry or deny that career. You will be able to serve Jesus better through it than without it. You will be able to use your skills, your expertise, your knowledge, as a way of serving him.

The world needs more dedicated and skilled Christian men and women in every area of life, in every profession, and every calling.

You will be a fisher of men just as effectively, even more effectively then, whether you use a bandage, a computer terminal, a drawing board, or a stick of chalk.

3. THEY WERE FISHERS OF MEN, NOT COLLECTORS OF PRINCIPLES

They followed a person, not a principle. Many people have principles instead of God. When the disciples got up and followed, they didn't follow a philosophy — a great idea that captured them. They didn't give their allegiance to a great ideology which they thought was 'the best thing since sliced bread.'

No, they just followed a person, a person whose over-riding love was for people — for them.

Always Jesus had a passion for people. He was individual orientated.

> If he spoke of a harvest, it was a human harvest.
> If he talked of a well, it was a well of living water to give life to people.
> If he spoke of things, they were always an analogy for human beings.
> He was a 'people person', not a 'system person'.

> Where other religious leaders saw buildings, govern-
> ments, laws, or codes of behaviour — Jesus saw
> people.

We here, as his followers, try to continue that emphasis.
The Church you have today joined is about relationships,
not regulations; it's about people, not principles; it's about
saints and sinners, not management systems. We welcome
you to our fellowship, assuring you that it's you as a person
God made, it's you as a person Christ died for, and it's you
as a person that we value.

If you've been to Hadrian's Wall, on the boundary of
England and Scotland, you'll know what a historic and
evocative thing it is. My theory is that Rome had enough of
Scottish Trade Union leaders and wanted to keep them out!

But if you have looked at all those old Roman altars and
monuments you'll have noted, as I did, that many of them
are dedicated to 'the genius of the place.' In the Roman
mind every place had its own god, its own spirit, its own
genius.

> We Christians follow a man, who is the genius of *every*
> place.
> Who knows where you will go in the years ahead?
> Who knows what you will be doing?
> Who knows what relationships you will form?

But one thing I can promise you. Jesus is the genius of
that place. There (wherever you are, and whomever you are
with) you will still hear that voice saying, 'Follow me, and I
will make you fishers of men'. In office, shop, courtroom,
hospital ward, factory, you will still see his beckoning finger.

And you will know that you are in a long line of committed
Christian men and women, following in the footsteps of
those first simple fishermen, and, still, after 2000 years,
being led on in his service.

May you follow him faithfully all your days, and may his
grace bless you richly in the years ahead.

7

ADULT BAPTISM/CHURCH MEMBERSHIP
THE PHEASANT

On my last holiday I spent some time feeding a tame pheasant. Like most people I've fed ducks at the local park with the children — I've fed geese and swans at wildfowl sanctuaries. (I find Canada geese the hungriest and the most tame.) I even remember giving an apple to a horse, and a bun to an elephant once at a zoo, but never before a pheasant. It was a male pheasant with a long colourful tail. He had a blue plastic ring round his leg, eyes like a microscope, and could see a biscuit crumb from 50 yards.

The interesting thing was that he was completely free. He could fly in or out, or even walk out of the caravan site where we were.

Yet he stayed with us, always within sight of where we were, and I couldn't help wondering why. After all he was a wild bird, as free as air. He had all that liberty, yet chose to stay. He had all that world of experiences out there, a few of which were known, many that were unknown, yet in spite of that, he made a decision to stay where he was.

As people, we have some areas of choice. Philosophers have a happy time arguing about it. Personally, I've given

up. I've settled for saying, 'I don't know what liberty is —
but I believe we have some, and I'm in favour of it!'

We are all constrained by the influences of our upbringing.
Our parents have brought us up the best way they know.
They taught us to clean our teeth, to be honest, to work,
learn and train. In between, they've given us their value
systems, for better or worse. We can rebel against them,
and youth is the time to do it, but there's no denying that
they're a powerful influence.

The environment in which we grow up affects us too. As
the years pass, we absorb the standards of the community,
the school, our peer group. It is possible to resist it, but it's
hard, because we're nearly all conformists in the end. The
desert is a lonely place and the voices crying in it are lonely
ones. Most of us acquiesce with what is expected of us.

But even so, I believe that we do have areas of free
choice — there do come times when the options are open,
the playing field is level — and we can freely decide, as my
pheasant did, and as you have today.

You have decided that the Christian pilgrimage is for
you, that you have been captured by the way Jesus looks at
you, by what he did for you, and by the standards he has
set for you. All of us rejoice in that commitment you have
made. We, too, have seen that vision, heard that call, and
responded to his commission.

I still wonder why that pheasant chose to stay!

They're not very bright as birds go — but I can think of
reasons which would make sense even to that birdbrain.

First, because it was known and recognized and valued.
That's the message of the ring round its leg. Somebody had
taken the trouble to catch it, and probably weigh it, examine
it, put the ring on its leg, and enter the number in a log book.

It's interesting to think of all the times that Jesus emphasized our value in God's sight as individuals. 'You are of
more value than even odd sparrows hopping on the
ground,' is one thing he said.' He also said, 'God cares for
you more than the lilies of the field.' 'Even the number of
hairs on our head are numbered,' is another. (Not a tremen-

dous job in the case of most ministers!) You are certainly of far greater value than a pheasant!

Jesus was convinced that God values each one of us, probably at a higher value than we value ourselves. There's a corner of his great mysterious love that's expressly reserved for each one of us, an area of his heart kept open for you.

I think that's partly why you have made your choice today, and why most of us stay within the Church. It's because within the Christian community we can remind ourselves that God knows us, values us, and loves us. We try, as best we can, to reflect that in our relationships with each other.

And you, now, can go anywhere in this world, as a converted and committed Christian, walk into any church of whatever country or culture, hold out your hand in greeting, and say, 'I'*m a Christian*,' and know that you should be welcomed as a colleague, a sharer in the work, a fellow-citizen of the Kingdom of God.

I reckon it stayed in that camp site for another reason. It was there that it was fed. In my experience, it much preferred Rich Tea biscuits. The people in the next door caravan emptied crumbs out of their door after every meal. That pheasant had eyes like a hawk, and suddenly appeared whenever they did it, and even faster when I went outside with my packet of biscuits. It knew where it was well off. None of this business of rooting through the hedgerows for rough old bits of anything like any run-of-the-mill pheasant — supermarket Rich Tea, that's what it was after.

I reckon that's what you have found out, and why the rest of us come here week by week. Because it's here that we are fed.

I remember a sermon by a minister who was being considered for an appointment. It was a very rousing evangelical appeal. He had the congregation laughing, and almost crying. There wasn't really much substance to it, it didn't really say anything, and nobody went away with anything to think about — just what an interesting preacher he was. It was a masterly example of how to stir a congregation of people.

I also remember the old minister who heard it all, and had a word with him at the door, 'Remember my lad, a congregation's like a tea cup — you have to fill it before your stir it.'

There are too many churches in our land filled with people suffering from arrested theological development — starved of the real meat of the Gospel. It's nice to have the odd fizzy drink or packet of crisps, but you can't live on them. Too many Christians are living on junk food, and are not grappling with the tremendous implications of what the Christian faith means for them. It's a pilgrimage of the mind and soul — a voyage of discovery into deep water. Too many Christians are hugging the shore, paddling in the shallow certainties.

The good Lord gave us minds, judgement, the ability to ponder, the facility to make jumps of imaginative insight, the talent to think, and he doesn't wish us to bury that talent in the sand. So read big books, think about the big issues, be prepared to make big decisions, and to change your minds.

Jesus's last command to Peter, and by implication to all leaders of the Church, was, if you remember, 'Feed my sheep,' and that's what any church worth its salt tries to do.

Wherever you may move to in the years ahead, attend a church for a few weeks to be stirred if you like, but make your permanent spiritual home somewhere where you and yours will be fed, and where your spiritual growth will be fostered and encouraged.

Why did our pheasant stay there when he could have walked up the path and across the road in front of a lorry at any time? It could have flown anywhere it chose. But it stayed where it was safe, and in its little brain it must have known that.

Out there it could have been run over, shot with a twelve bore, grabbed by a fox; all sorts of dangers lurked 100 yards up the road, but it knew that if it stayed there in the camp site the only danger it faced was of severe indigestion and colic from an overdose of Rich Tea biscuits.

One thing I can promise you is that, as a follower of Jesus, you will always feel safe. That's one of the reasons we are Christians too.

You'll have your share of sorrows and sufferings — problems and difficulties. Life is full of little Calvarys and little Resurrections — no-one is exempt from them. Our faith isn't any sort of complimentary pass out of real life. And these things will hurt you as much as they hurt anyone else.

But you'll know that you're in good hands because you will have one great advantage, you'll have someone with you — someone who's been through it himself, and knows what it feels like, and will accompany you safely through it.

Matthew records Jesus' last word to the disciples, 'I am with you always, even to the end of the world.' That's a very weak translation. Matthew actually used a couple of words that are much stronger: *Every day*. But even that is too weak. *Every* in the Greek word has the implication of wholeness, of totality, of completeness. *Absolutely every* is about as near as we can get in English.

The best translation I can find is from Barclay's New Testament. He says, 'And there is not a day when I will not be with you to the end of time.'

There lies our safety. There is nothing, as Paul said, that can separate us from the love of God in Christ Jesus. No road we can tread without him to guide us however dark it may be. No pitfall we can stumble into without him kneeling beside us to see if we're all right. No joy in our lives which does not put a smile on his face. We are safe.

So that pheasant which walked up to me on holiday, spoke, if it only knew it, of great eternal realities.

It points us to the reasons for committing our lives to Christ in the first place and, as the years pass, it gives us reasons for rededicating ourselves to the Lord who knows and loves us, who feeds us with the living bread, and who will be with us until our journey's end.

8
ADULT BAPTISM/CHURCH MEMBERSHIP
CALLED TO BE WHOLE

These days it isn't fashionable to belong to things, be it a political party, a pressure group or a church. Many of us are wary about signing up — committing ourselves. Perhaps it's something to do with modern life and modern attitudes. The old easy acceptance of authority, the agreement to abide by the rules, seems to have gone — we are more individualistic people these days. And although we are willing to support, to vote, to sign petitions, we don't so easily belong.

Which is an odd attitude, and not very logical. Because we all have a need to belong. We need to feel accepted and integrated.

We are ourselves, of course; one will, one mind, one set of drives and impulses in one personality and one body. We need to be ourselves and only ourselves. We need to call upon our inward resources to meet the problems of life. We need to see our own limits and know what we can and cannot do. We need to feel responsible, need to be able to choose, need a point from which things originate.

And yet with all this we also need to be forgiven for things we've done wrong, we need to be assured that we've done enough, tried enough, succeeded enough. We need

to feel fulfilled and complete, to be affirmed and accepted.
We need to belong.

Psychiatrists call it *affirming acceptance*. Ordinary people
like us call it *wholeness*. The Bible calls it *holiness*.

We want to be balanced, integrated, harmonious, whole
people. And what I want to say now is that belonging to the
Christian community which we call the Church does just
that.

Firstly, what the Christian faith does is to take the faults,
frailties and wrongness inside us, and puts them all in a
pardonable frame where they can be dealt with, like the old
poultices which we older ones among us had slapped on to
us when we were young. Hot kaolin poultices, remember
them? They draw all the poison out, and then clear it away.

It insists that, 'all have sinned and come short of the
glory of God,' and then insists just as strongly that, 'Christ
died to save us from our sins.'

None of us can look back and say we've never done anything we've been ashamed of. These memories can poison
our minds, and cripple our actions if we let them. So in
pointing to them, drawing them out, faith can put us in a
situation where they can be pardoned, and we can be
made whole.

So we end up not as perfect people, but as forgiven sinners. We sorrow over our sins, we accept our shortcomings,
but we are not weighed down by them, and our actions are
not inhibited by them. And we can't cast the first stone at
others' shortcomings, because we are too familiar with our
own.

Belonging to Christ, and the Christian community, can do
that.

Secondly, we all feel the need to send down roots. When
our latest grandson was christened, I handed him a family
heirloom. When I was born one of my grandfathers gave me
a half-sovereign. My mother, sensibly didn't spend it but
saved it and gave it to me when I was old enough to appreciate it. So, at my grandson's christening, I gave it to him in
the hope that he'll give it to his grandson when the time
comes. After all, he will need, as we all need, a sense of

personal history, a world view in which we have our place —
roots of our own.

In our Church we have a great tradition, national and
local. And this long history is a rich saga of great adventure
and faith. These roots are now yours.

When I arrived here some years ago and found that I had
to speak to the Women's Meeting on the first Monday of
every month, I wondered what on earth I'd be able to say
on all those occasions. Well, I've done it, and never
repeated myself. And I'll tell you how I do it. I look up the
stories of the pioneers of the Church, and particularly in this
area. I've never run short.

*(Names of the founders of the church, pioneers of Christianity in the
area.)*

I've never got near to running out of stories of men and
women like these. They are part of our tradition, our history.
That's just our local history, think of all the centuries before
that, and the places away from here. Faithful, adventurous,
thrilling roots, which we are happy to share with any who
join us.

We all need, like dandelion seeds, to plant our feet, to
cease drifting in the wind, to reach solid earth, and are not
complete until we do.

Belonging to Christ, and the Christian community, can do
that.

We welcome you for what you bring to our fellowship,
your insights and character, your gifts and graces, even your
faults and frailties. Because we always try to thank God that
the thorns have roses on them, rather than blame him
because the roses have thorns on them. We welcome and
accept you for what you are.

We hope that within the Church family you will feel the
stimulus and encouragement to personal growth and development. You will find, I'm sure, that we all have a great deal
that we can learn with and from each other.

For what the fellowship can offer to you, we welcome
you. As for the traditions of the past, we are happy to share
them with you so that you can make them your own.

As for the sense of family we have, the care and warmth

which is so often seen among us, we are happy to share this with you.

As for the deep underlying Christian beliefs, which Paul called the 'Mysteries of the faith,' God's love, God's goodness and God's grace, we are trying to make them live among us, and with your help, perhaps, we can do it even better.

We welcome you who now belong.

Now to Him who is able to do immeasurably more than all we ask or imagine, according to His power that is at work within us, to Him be glory in the Church and in Christ Jesus throughout all generations, for ever and ever, Amen.

9

ADULT BAPTISM/CHURCH MEMBERSHIP

ME AND US

The glory of our Christian faith is that it reaches deeper than our minds can comprehend, and is more profound than our hearts can feel. If we lived a hundred lifetimes we wouldn't be able to fully understand it. As a way into truth, as an approach to reality, I believe it is more incisive and more true than any other world view.

What intrigues me is the way that truth never seems to be clear-cut, being in one thought or another, but is found in a tension between two or more thoughts. In this case, Oscar Wilde was right when he said of the pure and simple truth that, 'the truth is rarely pure, and never simple.' The Christian often has to hold two opposing truths in tension. Neither is right, and neither is wrong, the truth lies in the tension between the two. If you stretch a rubber band between your hands, and imagine that each hand is one idea, the truth lies in the twang!

This is truly borne out as we think of this significant service when we receive you into the body of Christian believers which is the Christian Church.

One of the truths is clear. Our faith is an individual thing. It's a one-to-one personal relationship with God. God has many children in this world, something over 5,000 million, people say. But he doesn't have any grandchildren at all! We can't inherit our relationship with God, we can't get it by proxy, or win it by luck in a prize draw. It's an inward response that we make to God of ourselves and by ourselves. You have made this response as an individual. You have said, 'Yes, count me in.'

Harry Fosdick told the story of a little German village, and in that village a humble house where the schoolmaster lived. Over the doorway he had carved these proud words, 'Dante, Molière, and Goethe live here.' He was obviously a good schoolmaster, because those great giants of literature weren't just names to him, but real companions who inspired him.

St Paul said something similar, 'I live, yet not I, but Christ lives in me.' If a schoolmaster can say that Dante, Molière and Goethe can live in him, surely Paul can say, and we can say, that Christ lives in us. That one-to-one relationship is at the heart of all Christian discipleship. Whether it has come as a blinding Damascus Road experience at a particular time and place, or as a slowly growing yet irresistible compulsion, that personal experience is an essential element in our service today.

That is the truth represented by one end of the stretched rubber band.

But it is also true that we are saved in community, and we can't be saved by ourselves. We can be individual Christians, but never isolated ones. For we are now members of a pilgrim group, travelling, like the wandering tribes of Israel, through the wilderness. Separated from the group, we are lost and we perish. There are, of course, a wide variety of pilgrim groups travelling along slightly different paths to the same destination, but we must trudge along with one or other of them if we are to get to the other end safely. When we are footsore and weary, others will help us along, and when our companions need our help we must give it. That's what pilgrims do.

There's an old Easter legend which says that the gate of heaven is so narrow that one person walking alone can't get through. Two people side by side can just manage it. But when ten people, each of them helping the other, try to enter, the gate is so wide, you can't see the sides.

We belong, all of us now, to this Christian community. We are members of it. We've made it our spiritual home. We all take part of the blame for its bad points and failings, we each swell a bit with pride over its achievements and virtues. There is a community angle to our salvation that we lose at our peril.

The Church is never a place, but always a people — never a fold, but always a flock, never a sacred building, but always a believing group. The Church is we who pray, not where we pray. The structure in which we worship, made of stone and brick, wood and slate, can never be a Church, any more than your clothes can ever be you. The true Temple of God, as Paul pointed out, is in our hearts and in our collective life.

The joint experience of Christian people has an inspiration and validity of its own. 'I believe in the holy Catholic Church' is not only a phrase in the creed, it is part of the Gospel — part of the good news itself.

That's the other end of the rubber band. We are saved in community. I know that in this day and age it's not popular to say such things. Today, individualism is held up as the ultimate good, and a politician could say, 'there's no such thing as society.' But I'm not concerned with what is fashionable today, but what is true. I'm not bothered about being politically correct, I'm far more interested in being theologically correct. And of this I am sure. The big words — the really big words in the Christian vocabulary — like Father, Kingdom, Love, Reconciliation, are all community words. Yes, we are individuals, but individuals who are in community. And in the tension between these two truths, lies our salvation.

Today, you and we all, commit and recommit ourselves to the Lord we try to serve. We set out again as a pilgrim group on the unknown path to the Commonwealth of God of which we are citizens — rededicated, refreshed, and ready to follow. And praying for God's strength and guidance upon us all.

10
ADULT BAPTISM/CHURCH MEMBERSHIP
PERFECT FREEDOM

Thomas Cranmer, in one of his inspired prayers wrote of God, 'whose service is perfect freedom.' A strange paradox! To serve someone full-time, to be at someone else's beck and call, is not to be able to call your time your own. It is to do what they want, rather than what you want. And yet Cranmer calls this service 'perfect freedom'. In so doing, he put his finger on a profound truth, which is at the root of all Christian discipleship, and certainly at the heart of what we are doing in this service.

In the days of the Cold War, when the Communists held down Eastern Europe with an iron fist, there was the story of a Hungarian who applied to emigrate to the West.

'Why do you want to emigrate?' they asked him, 'Aren't you happy?' 'I've no complaints!' the man replied. 'Are you dissatisfied with your work?' 'I've no complaints,' was the answer. 'Are you discontented with your living conditions?' 'No complaints.' 'Well, for goodness sake, why do you want to emigrate to the West?' 'Well,' he replied, 'because there I can have complaints!'

Here in the West we have freedom to complain, among many other freedoms, thank God. But it isn't perfect freedom, is it? Because we are constricted by things we take for granted. I may have the freedom to travel to Polynesia, and spend six months lazing under a palm tree. (What a lovely thought!) But, in fact, I can't, because I have to work, and my diary won't let me. I may theoretically have the freedom to go into a car showroom and buy the latest model Jaguar. But in practice I can't, because my bank account won't let me.

My freedom is restricted by my circumstances, and so is yours. We may have every opportunity to walk into a travel agent and book a flight to Polynesia and there's no law preventing us from ordering a new Jaguar. But we can't, because we're restricted not by outside laws, but by what we are.

So when we talk of 'perfect freedom', we are visualizing a liberty from inward restrictions, as well as outward laws. The freedom to do these things as well as the freedom to choose them.

Of course, freedom is a great New Testament word. That's not surprising, for slavery was the bedrock of the Roman Empire and was even known to a lesser extent among the Jews themselves.

Jesus, in the synagogue, read from the scroll of Isaiah, 'The Lord has sent me to preach good news to the poor, has sent me to proclaim freedom to the prisoners.'

John records Jesus saying to the Jews, 'If the Son of God makes you free, you shall be free indeed.'

Paul picks the subject up in his letter to the Romans, 'Where the spirit of the Lord is, there is liberty.'

Liberty, freedom, are great biblical words, and profound biblical themes. In some paradoxical way, God emancipates us, he breaks our chains, he sets us free. Surrounded as we are by our nature, our influences, our constrictions, our pressures, God gives us moments of stark open choice.

He gives us the freedom to reach higher than we could on our own, to be better people than in our own strength we could achieve. He gives us the liberty to actually get that break in Polynesia or own that Jaguar — spiritually speaking. The inward chains which have bound us down are broken.

What holds us down so often is ourselves. The burden of

our past attitudes and prejudices. The blindness of our lack of sympathy and discernment. The shackles of an inward-turning selfishness. The shadows of guilt for past actions. All these things are restrictions on our freedom; they're our own personal handcuffs, and God can break their tethers and set us free.

This points to the central paradox, the only way God can do this for us is when we give our liberty to him. The only way to keep our freedom is to give it away — to see the finger of Jesus beckoning, to hear his voice saying, 'follow me'. The only way to get perfect freedom is to surrender to him our limited freedom. It means to make his will ours, his purposes ours, his aims our own, his methods our guide, complete surrender of our freedom of action.

And in the mystery of God, in this surrender we find our victory, in this bondage our liberty. We are then free to achieve the best, not just the worst. We are free to live the life of the next world, as well as this. We shall then prove in our own experience that God's service is indeed perfect freedom, and we shall know for ourselves that when we find God we find our liberty, and when we lose him we lose that too.

This you have done today. We rejoice that we have you now as partners in our Christian community. You take upon you the obligations that we share here, and shoulder them, as we all do. You'll find these duties, we hope, a delight. You join a fellowship where we are constantly discovering new avenues of service, experiencing ever more pain and pleasure in loving our neighbours, continually being surprised by God's love.

You are now citizens in the Commonwealth of God, where we are all free, free at last. Free to reach into the fathomless love of God, free to scale the heights of our own personal spiritual development, free to be what we all, in our best moments, would wish in God's sight to be. And in his service, find perfect freedom.

| |

WEDDING

TO LOVE

I've an opportunity at this point in the service to have a few words of my own, and I confess I'm a little hesitant. For one thing there's the common caricature of the parson who lives in so rarefied an atmosphere that we don't know what marriage is all about. Or that we're so sexless that we'd have trouble cross-breeding geraniums.

However, I'll carry on, because there are plenty of old married hands here who will tell you whether I'm talking sense or not.

What I want to tell you, (Bride), and you, (Groom), is that you'll go through three stages in your marriage — if you're lucky.

FIRST, YOU'LL REALIZE THAT THERE'S ONLY ONE KIND OF LOVE

It's a total attitude that you have to each other — and it's lovely. It's a romantic cloud, emotional candyfloss; it's looking into each other's eyes every five minutes; it's undoing the wedding present and saying, 'How lovely, yet another cruet set;' it's blushing when someone calls you Mrs (Groom's surname); it's saying, 'I'll consult my wife'; it's a totally fizzy feeling; it's feeling woozy when you're stone cold sober; it's realizing that the steam rising from the pizza isn't steam at all but the shade of Barbara Cartland. And it's lovely!

Your loving relationship is all of a piece, as indeed it ought to be — at the beginning.

AND THEN

I'll give you six months, and then you'll realize that you both have faults which have to be allowed for and forgiven. It was once said that a happy marriage is the union of two good forgivers. You'll realize that you both have limitations which have to be accepted, and irritating little habits which have to be changed. In short, you'll come up against the fact that neither of you is perfect, and so you won't have a perfect marriage either.

I heard of one woman who was invited to take the man 'for better and for worse', and she replied 'Well, he won't get much better, and he can't get much worse — so I'll take him as he is.'

Then you'll realize that there's not just one kind of love but several different sorts. There's the romantic love which you get on a warm starlit night when you're out for a meal, just the two of you. It still comes, however the years pass, I'm glad to say.

Then there's the friendly love — the liking that's based on the sharing of confidences, interests and experiences, the partnership which will ease the way for both of you. Don't underrate that kind of love. There's truth in the old Czech proverb which says, 'Don't choose your partner at a dance, but in the fields among the harvesters.'

Then there's the deep commitment of love deeper than feeling or romance, more profound than partnership. The New Testament kind of love which you have pledged to each other today. That love which is the keynote of Christian relationships, and especially the characteristic of a Christian marriage.

Yes, you'll realize soon that there are many kinds of love.
Each of them will present you with its own challenges, each
will make its own demands, each will reward you with its
particular joys.

AND THEN

I'll give you a couple of years — if you're good — and then
you'll discover something else, that there is really in the
end only one kind of love after all. You'll find that each
variety of love is affected, conditioned and strengthened
by the others. And that between them they'll give you a
glimpse of something very profound and cosmic.

You know what it's like when you drive along a lane
between the hedges, or travel in a fast-moving train. You
get, for a few brief moments, the sight of a wonderful view.
You see a broad sunlit scene, and then the houses and the
hedges get in the way, and it's gone.

Well, at the noblest and most humbling moments of your
love you will catch, through cracks in your worldliness,
glimpses of the panorama of God's love. You will see flashing
insights into the paradoxical world of a love greater than
you have ever known. And in the sunlight perhaps you will
see, on a small hill, an empty cross, and children will be
dancing round it. You will realize the depths of sacrificial
love that Jesus taught to people, the quality of love in the
life he lived, and how this divine love was reflected in
everything he was.

The Apostle John said in his first letter, 'whoever lives in
love, lives in God.' You will see your love as a small particle
of a great truth, your relationship as a line in an eternal
story; you will see, breaking into your town and your time,
the universal and timeless love of God.

I hope your marriage will grow in depth as it should in
the days to come. May the first stage be full of romance, the
second be full of interest, and the best stage be full of
inspiration.

May you, (*Bride*), always find in (*Groom*) 'your very parfait gentle knight,' to use Chaucer's words. And, (*Groom*), may (*Bride*) always look in your eyes as young and charming as she looks today. God bless you both.

12
WEDDING
TO CHERISH

My first words must be those of congratulation, and hope that you'll find in your life together all the good things you wish for yourselves. I was at a wedding reception last week and a lady guest was standing by me as we looked at the happy couple. 'D'you think they know what marriage is all about?' she asked me. 'No,' I said, 'but they'll soon find out!' Well, so will you. Sometimes I put texts on our notice board at the church entrance. I haven't got a copy of 'Father forgive them for they know not what they do.' Which is just as well — I'd be sorely tempted. But at least you know enough about each other to want to spend your lives together, and that's good. My hope is that all the new discoveries you make about each other will be happy surprises, and not sudden shocks, and that as time goes by your love, as the service says, 'will grow and deepen with the years.'

One of the solemn pledges you have made today is to 'love and cherish' each other. That's a lovely word 'cherish'. I looked up the definition in the dictionary.

TO CHERISH = TO NURSE

All right we're grown up, adult, independent people, but there still come times for all of us when we need to lean on someone else. Life can be tough, and continual problems are sometimes the only prospect we can see. It's no use people trying to kid you that your marriage will be nothing but success and happiness ever after — we all know that life isn't like that. There are bound to be times when everything seems to go wrong, when your view will be nothing but dark clouds. When that happens you'll need to be able to lean on each other's strength.

To cherish each other as you've promised is to be that prop to each other when you need it, the emotional strength when disappointments submerge your partner, the encourager when the other is tempted to give up, the supplier of sympathy and understanding when no-one else can do either.

In old fashioned marriages the husband was seen as the strong man, and the wife the weak little thing who had to be protected. I doubt if that was ever the real state of affairs, it certainly isn't so now. Strength doesn't necessarily go with size. Wendell Wilkie was a great public orator, but his wife was really the power behind the throne. Whenever he left the house she would straighten his tie and say, 'Now Wendell, remember what I said, don't shilly-shally.'

Cherishing and nursing each other isn't a one-way thing. For you're both human, and you'll both need to be surrounded by the love and care of each other. You'll both need to learn the art of nursing each other from the wounds that life brings, and set each other up on your feet again — fit to face the world. It's not only children who benefit from being kissed better. That's part of what cherishing each other means.

TO CHERISH = TO KEEP WARM

When a gardener cherishes a precious plant, he makes sure it's kept warm. When a mother cherishes a baby she does the same. In a marriage it's not just physical but emotional warmth that matters. Don't shut up your feelings inside yourselves, because that leads to barriers of pretence, and can destroy your marriage. Be at ease with yourself so that you can be at ease with each other.

May you want to go home, not because all your things are there, but because the warmth of your partner is there — because you'll know that when you go in the door you'll be greeted with respect, liking, friendship and love, and not like Norah Batty, with a yard brush. After a while it may not be very obvious, or demonstrative, but it'll be there I trust, and you'll know it. So even when the central heating has broken, and you lie in bed with your wife's icy feet in your back, may you still feel wrapped in the warmth of each other's affection. May you feel cherished.

TO CHERISH = TO HOLD IN ONE'S HEART

The relationship you begin today is the deepest commitment one human being can give to another. It goes to the roots of what we are. This is what makes a Church wedding different from a Register Office one. There you don't make promises, here you do. There it's a matter of accepting each other. Here it's a matter not just of acceptance, but of a deep and life-long level of commitment. And that's what will make your marriage a Christian one — whether you can hold that level of committed love to each other. Whether you can look at Jesus, and live out that quality of self-giving love between you.

To 'hold in one's heart' is as nice a definition of it as one can have; to be thinking about each other often when you're apart; to have a good day when your partner achieves something good; to be down when the other fails; to share each other's hopes, ambitions, and reactions, as if they are happening to you; to hold in your heart.

I heard of one wedding where, when the minister held the book out for the Best Man to put the rings on, the Best Man, who had quite a past, put his hand on the book and said automatically, 'I swear to tell the truth, the whole truth, and nothing but the truth.'

Well, marriage is when your partner knows the truth about you and still loves you anyway. Someone once said that loving relationships are our best protection against the challenges of the world, and I reckon that's true. One of the finest things in life, and the best things in marriage, is to know that you are held in your partner's heart — that you're cherished.

Actually, the word is used in Shakespeare — *Romeo and Juliet*, no less. Juliet says, 'Yet I should kill thee with much cherishing!' Well, if you'll take my advice you'll run the risk.

May you love and cherish each other until you reach your 75th anniversary, and then may you consider the situation and decide you want to go on. May you, (Groom), be satisfied with having bowled your best maiden over. And may you, (Bride), enjoy the experience of being for at least one of your audience, always the leading lady.

In other words, God bless you both.

13
WEDDING
'I WILL'

A few moments ago you said those fateful and significant words, 'I will'

You, (*Groom*), could have said, 'I *won't*', turned round and gone home — but you didn't. It *would* have cast rather a damper on the day. In spite of what everybody says about Bridegrooms, I think they *would* have missed you!

When I said, (B*ride*), 'Will you have this man,' you could have said, 'yes please,' but that would have shown a rather unseemly enthusiasm, and you didn't.

In the old service the question was, 'wilt thou?' to which the obvious answer is, 'I have already wilted thank you.'

But in fact you both stuck to the words of the service and said, 'I *will*' nicely and accurately in the right place. Legally, of course, it's your statement that what you are doing is of your own free will. Nobody's standing behind you daring you to duck out. Nobody's pressurizing you into marrying each other. It's your decision, and you're going through with it.

Because, when you think of it, marriage is an enormous step to take; it's the deepest decision in the realm of relationships that a human being can ever make. You've decided that you want to spend the rest of your lives sharing the experiences of life, it's joys and sorrows, together. You have faced and overcome the normal barriers with which we protect ourselves from other people.

As we all know, there's a natural reticence and privacy in our lives. We safeguard ourselves against being hurt by others by putting on a public face, a surface shell. By saying, 'I will' you have agreed to drop that outward crust with each other — to allow one other person into that inner sanctum of your feelings, to know you as you really are. You are allowing yourself to be very vulnerable to one other person.

That demands a great deal of trust in each other and a lot of nervousness and doubts to overcome. And so you have reached the point of being able to say with honesty and sincerity, 'I will'. In doing this, in your own way and in the privacy of your inner thoughts, you have each won a personal battle.

I know that you have thought about this deeply, and you know that life isn't a 'happy ever after' thing, but a journey that's a mixture of joys and sorrows. And many of these joys and sorrows, indeed the most intense of them, are not to do with things, but with people, and with relationships. Yet, you defy these thoughts, and with a cheerful confidence you place your future happiness in your partner's hands. You have posted each other, like sentries, to guard your inner happiness.

Your 'I will' is a great affirmation of faith and trust in each other. You can't prove that your partner will live up to that trust. You are putting your faith in each other. And the rest of us see a touch of nobility in that, and something rather beautiful.

A lot of the time, we don't live life, life lives us. Our diaries and our purses tell us what we can and can't do. Then there's what other people expect. How we live is so often dictated not by what we want, but by what is expected of us — the assumptions of other people, the needs the wider community has from us, the roles we find ourselves in — it's difficult sometimes to see just where what *we* want fits in.

You have said today, of your own free choice, 'I will'. It's one of those rare times when we can really exercise what we want. A wedding is an occasion of joy. Joy that human beings can do such things. That you can from your own freedom, and with clear eyes, bind yourself to one other person so closely, and say:

This is what we've decided, with determination and purpose, WE WILL.

Now this isn't a religious thing in the strict sense of the word. Touching, deep, profound — yes, but on a strictly human level.

But by solemnizing your marriage in this church, and, as we believe, in the presence of God, and asking his blessing on it, you are doing much more.

For there is a third person who has to answer the question, 'Will you?', and it's God. He has a great deal to do with the happiness of your marriage.

Your new home will be a class in his school, for every family is a seminar where we learn to love others — a teaming up for the pilgrimage of life, which has him as our destination. Yes, his 'I will' is very important on a day like this. And his 'I will' crowns your decision, and makes it part of his purposes. His 'I will' turns your wedding into the Holy Estate of Marriage.

Fortunately, those who know God well, know that his favourite word is '*yes*', and his nature is to be creative and loving. He demonstrated his love by creating us, and sending his Son to lift us up to his level of love. You can be assured that by bringing your relationship into this place and into the atmosphere of worship to have it blessed, your 'I will' has been echoed by God's 'I will'. Your new family isn't just a unit in the government statistics, but a foundation block in God's kingdom.

Your love comes from each other, but that love will be reverberated and deepened by God's love. And the strength of that love will keep you going when your own falters.

In this place today, God has joined you together, and what God has joined let no human being or agency separate.

So we wish you every blessing from this day on, and our prayer is that his love will warm your home.

God bless you both.

14

WEDDING

THE MARRIAGE PARADOX

My first word must be one of congratulation to you both. It is all our wishes that you'll have a long and happy married life together.

Marriage is a paradox. A strange blend of contradictory things.

In one way it's a sinking of yourself in your partner — a willing suspension of what *you* want to do as an individual, or what *you* want to be as a person, so that you can immerse yourself in your partner's life.

One symbol of this that we've just seen is the joining of your hands. We've done this as a sign of oneness, of togetherness, or unity. 'The two shall be one flesh,' as the Bible says — whatever may come, sadnesses, sorrows, challenges, choices. With love and laughter you'll rise above them hand in hand.

It's a bit like climbing a mountain, where you go in twos. One holds the rope while the other climbs upward, then that one holds the rope for the other to clamber higher.

We've seen in our marriage preparation groups that success in marriage isn't about what happens to you both, but whether you can face and tackle whatever happens together, as a team.

As the poet says,

'a brief intense forgetting of self,
a leap away from the "me".'

Many people whose marriages have broken up, look back, and find that it's because one or both of them thought they could be married and remain single. Marriage isn't about living life as if you're on your own, with a husband or wife 'bolted on'. It needs a completely new approach; you have to learn to think in terms of two and not one; of pleasing your partner and not just yourself. Yes, marriage is about joining hands — it's about partnership.

It's from this sharing and joining that the joys and the sorrows come.

Yet this is where the paradox comes in. For marriage is also the highlighting of you as an individual person.

You will be a much more important person, a significant person, a vital person to at least one other. Depended upon more, relied upon more. More demands will be made upon you than ever before. You will be forced to become a much more mature person. It is, in fact, your last chance to grow up because your partner has appointed you to several new roles. Take just a couple of them.

YOU ARE THE GUARDIAN OF YOUR PARTNER'S SOLITUDE

You both need your times alone, you both need your private space — your own secret world into which, for your own peace of mind, you need to withdraw sometimes. You will need breathing spaces, times to sit and think without pressure, opportunity to ponder, space to recreate your own poise.

Without these spaces life becomes a mad rush, and we end up *doing* everything and *being* nothing. These times are important psychologically and spiritually for you both.

In the New Testament we read that even in the busy

hectic life that Jesus lived, he took every chance he could to get away from the crowds to meditate and pray.

You have appointed each other today to the very responsible positions of guardians of each other's solitude.

YOU ARE TODAY APPOINTED AS PROTECTORS OF EACH OTHER'S INTEGRITY

Deep inside both of you are feelings that you find difficult to express. They're the inward motivations and responses that you feel would only be laughed at if you raised them in a pub or at work. Yet they're what you really feel, and you've never expressed them to anyone else. To do that would make you much too vulnerable. And yet, those are the deep down things which make you tick. They are what make you do things which surprise people who think they know you well.

You now have someone to whom you can confide all these feelings, without any danger. You can really open your heart to one other person, knowing that you'll not be laughed at, but will be listened to with sympathy and honesty.

In the life of Jesus we see that he, too, had his close group of special people, with whom he could be open and share what he felt.

What you have done today is to appoint your partner as the protector of your integrity, as you are the protector of your partner's.

They are just two new roles you have as separate people — there are many others.

And so, in this strange way, marriage raises both our togetherness and our individuality. And it challenges us in both areas to rise to new abilities and qualities.

It's my wish and prayer, and that of all your relations and friends here today that you'll both respond to and achieve the things we've thought about today, and that as a result your marriage will be a long, happy, and fulfilled one.

May the strangers who meet you, (Bride), in the years

ahead see on your face as well as on your finger the signs of a happy marriage, and may you, (*Groom*), demonstrate quite clearly by your inner poise and your expanding waistline that you have a loving wife.

May God bless you both.

15

WEDDING

THE THING THAT LASTS

As you heard in our Bible reading, 'In this life we have three great lasting qualities, faith, hope and love. But the greatest of them is love.'

The last time I was leaving the United States, the folk at the church I was at showered me, as those generous and warm-hearted people always do, with small parting gifts. One of them was a tooth. Not an ordinary tooth, a mastodon tooth. The predecessor of the elephant was a mammoth, and the one before that was a mastodon — an enormous thing like an elephant but twice as big. Anyway, they gave me the tooth. 'Just what I always wanted,' I said. Well, you have to be polite!

So I travelled back with this, hoping that the customs wouldn't query it. It's the oldest thing I own — 3 million years old. The rest of the mastodon has long decayed away, even the great bones have dissolved into dust. But its teeth survived.

In marriage some things don't survive.

The bright shiny newness of your wedding presents will wear off pretty quickly. China gets broken; electrical gadgets will in time end with a purple flash and an acrid smell; furnishings will shrink, tear, fade, or have unmentionable things spilled on them. You'll end up like the rest of us, in 40 years' time, with just one or two precious things you can point at and say, 'They were wedding presents.' *Things* don't last.

You are, I am sure, convinced at this moment that you're marrying the perfect husband or wife. Well, it won't take you long to discover that you aren't. There's nothing like being married to someone to find out what they're really like. And you'll discover that the person you're married to is a human being, with faults as well as virtues, with failings and irritating little habits, as well as good and kind things.

It's just as well your promises have been 'for worse as well as better, in sickness as well as in health.'

That lovely wedding day romance, that blue bird twittering, that sweeping of confetti out of impossible places, that twinkle in everybody's eyes on a day like this — make the most of it — enjoy it — because it won't last.

What will last are the things that St Paul described. 'In this life we have three great lasting qualities. Faith, Hope and Love, and the greatest of them is love.'

When St Paul and his Cypriot friend Barnabas walked round the south coast of Cyprus 2000 years ago, he passed by Aphrodite's Rock. That was where the Greeks said the Goddess of Love was washed ashore on a seashell. I saw it a few years ago at sunset — what a sight! On the hill above the rock was Aphrodite's temple, where there were all sorts of physical goings on in the name of the Goddess of Love.

And it was about this time that Paul wrote the words of our reading today. He put together a definition of love that's a world away from the superficial love he saw there. It was the sort of love that he saw in the life of Jesus, a divine love.

Paul visualized a deep commitment between a man and a woman that is just as much to do with your will, your determination, and your mind, as with your bodies and your emotions. What he means isn't just physical attraction, but a total orientation of yourself to the well-being of your partner.

Now that *does* last. However the wedding presents break,

or the illusions fade, or the romance evaporates — the kind of Christian love that Paul describes goes on forever.

It's the one thing that still stands when all else falls away. Like my mastodon tooth, it can, in disastrous circumstances be the one thing that's left, as you stand together in the wreckage of your hopes. It can be the one source of light and warmth when darkness is all around.

> We two make home of any place we go,
> We two find joy in any kind of weather,
> If the earth is clothed in bloom or snow,
> If summer days invite, or bleak winds blow,
> What does it matter, if together
> We two, we two, make our world and our weather.

May your marriage be a success, may that love between you always be kept shining bright. May the love of God, of which your love is a part, be in your hearts and in your home.

May God bless you both.

16
WEDDING
TRUE RICHES

A man was talking to a monk once and asked what the three knots in his girdle were for. 'They signify poverty, chastity and obedience,' was the reply. 'Oh well, if you define chastity as being faithful to one's wife, then I could tie three knots in my belt as well,' said the man. 'I'm married, which is chastity, and the poverty and obedience follow naturally from that!'

Maybe we can leave the chastity and obedience for another occasion — let's talk about poverty. In a couple of hours' time people will be making lots of nice speeches and wishing you all sorts of things. I'm sure they'll be elegantly phrased. They won't be as blunt as I am going to be now. I'm not going to pussyfoot around. My wish for you in the years ahead is that you'll be rich. But rich in particular ways.

1. MAY YOU BE RICH IN YOUR AFFECTION FOR EACH OTHER

May you always feel warm in each other's company. May you always want to go home because of who is there, rather than where it is. May you always be able to exchange glances of common bond across a room, and agree without having to say a word. May you be able to be playful, and find a playmate in each other without being told to stop being silly. May there be a tingle in the shared tablecloth, and even a wonder in the washing-up.

May you be so full of affection that it will become a visible thing that others can see — and they will say, 'how rich you are.'

2. MAY YOU BE RICH IN YOUR RELATIONSHIPS

We hope that you'll be surrounded by a quiverful of children (to use that wonderful phrase from the Psalms), that in due time your family circle will be extended and your affection enlarged to include some little ones, who in decades to come will thank God for the stable, loving home into which they were born.

Incidentally, to bring up children well, my advice is to give them half as much money and twice as much time as you were going to in the first place.

Let your affection spill over into friendships. Hospitality is a great virtue. You'll remember Dickens' *Christmas Carol*. Who would you rather be? Ebenezer Scrooge, in lonely isolation, counting his money, or Bob Cratchet, surrounded by his family and friends, gathered round the fire? Be a Cratchet! Let warmth, generosity and hospitality be a keynote of your home.

And your friends will say, 'Well, we don't know what they've got in the bank, but in all the things that matter — they're rich!'

3. MAY YOU BE RICH IN YOUR PERCEPTIONS

May you be rich in your awareness of what other people don't see, or rather, don't notice:

> the mysterious reflections of leaves on still water;
> your partner's eyelashes after a bath;

the way a raindrop bends a blade of grass;

the soft tone of a woman's voice when she talks to a baby;

the sunlight glistening on a ladybird;

having a sentence of poetry or a tune ringing in your memory like a big bell;

hearing that bit from the Bible, 'God is Love,' and wondering at the way it works out in the life of Jesus;

the feeling of sacredness and timelessness you get in certain places like this.

These riches are under our noses all the time, riches of imagination, perception, depth, growth. Most people don't look very often, and their experience of life is poverty-stricken as a result.

I heard of a wife who saved £1000 over the years, which she spent on some luxury she wanted. This came as a complete surprise to her husband who couldn't think where she'd kept the money. 'I kept it in the family Bible,' she said. 'I knew it was the one place you'd never look!'

Our lives, our relationships, our families, are full of little treasures not yet discovered. Find them! Get off the tramlines of routine sometimes and look a bit harder at the things you take for granted.

Then you'll be fully alive, and the people who know you well will say, 'We don't know whether the house is paid for or not, but they're rich in spirit.'

So, to sum up my wishes for you: I hope you'll have enough money to get along comfortably. After all, as the saying goes, 'If your outgoings exceed your income, your upkeep will be your downfall.'

But most of all my wish for you is that you'll be rich in the real things that matter — the emotional and spiritual qualities that are at the heart of all good marriages.

May God bless you both.

17
WEDDING
SHARING

When we think about our relations and friends, we know them very well, of course, and sometimes they do things that are absolutely true to character. Though you've only now got married, you know each other well enough to know pretty broadly what to expect of each other. I expect that (Bride), you've seen (Groom) do something, and you've had a little secret smile to yourself, because it's just the thing he WOULD do. It's absolutely true to character. I dare say (Groom), you could say the same about (Bride). You can think of something she's done that's so typical of her, that it completely sums up the sort of person she is.

Well, it's human nature, and as old as history. It's in the New Testament, no less, and there's one event in Jesus' life that created such an impression on the Gospel writers, that all of them included it in their books — the same story repeated four times. They did it, because to them it was so significant and seemed to sum up all that Jesus stood for. It's the miracle of the Feeding of the Five Thousand. It's so typical of the sort of thing Jesus did, and still does in people's lives. And it's very applicable to a wedding, to *your* wedding. What hit the Gospel writers wasn't Jesus' mastery over the physical situation, they knew of that already, but the fact that the condition of the miracle was that he got a crowd of suspicious people sharing. There they were, sitting down (in groups or in rows, depending on which Gospel you read) and they shared. These Jews, so finicky about the purity of their kosher food, so particular about whom they ate with, shared food with people they didn't know, and with this sharing the blessing came.

Today, you two have given your lives to each other in the deepest act of sharing that human beings are capable of, and it is in your true sharing that God's blessing will come.

THE FIRST THING THAT THE DISCIPLES DID WAS ASK JESUS TO HELP

'Help! Lord, how are we going to feed this lot?'

There will come times in your marriage when even the two of you together come up against a problem you cannot solve. Disasters come to the best families and the worst. And sometimes we get to the end of our emotional, spiritual, and financial resources. In those situations, ask Jesus to help. It's the surest way to get through with your faith and your marriage intact. Ask him together, and he will give you his strength together. There's still a lot of truth in the old slogan, 'The Family that Prays Together Stays Together.' And I would add that it's not words that matter, but for both of you to spend time quietly together and realize the great eternal realities.

> We need wide spaces in our lives,
> Where faithful husbands, and loving wives,
> Can grow serene.
> Life gets so choked by busy living,
> Kindness so lost in fussy giving
> That God slips by unseen.

THEN WE HAVE TO OFFER WHAT WE HAVE

The starting point for the feeding of all those people was when a young lad offered what was in his lunch box. So often children show a simple generosity, which shames us adults. I've often wondered what his mother thought when he got home and explained what he'd eaten. 'What! When I only gave you five scones and two sardines!'

So in your marriage, as in everything else, the starting point of all his blessings is when we offer what we have first. Offer him your happiness, and find it doubly blessed. Offer him your relationship and find it filled with his grace. Offer him your limited horizons, and find them expanded into possibilities you can only dream of.

THE 5000 WERE FED BECAUSE THEY DID WHAT JESUS SAID

'Sit down here? What for?' they could have said. 'Share with these people? Certainly not!' they might have replied. But no, they did what he said, and were fed as a result.

In your individual lives up to now, you've tried to be 'obedient to the heavenly vision.' Now, as a married couple it's even more important. For your new opportunities and new responsibilities will bring fresh challenges and fresh temptations. You will have to rely even more heavily on the God who loves you, the Christ who saves you, and the Holy Spirit who guides you.

You have a wider circle of relations now, they'll be keeping a benevolent eye on you for a start. Then there are any new (*Groom's surname*)s who might appear; they'll be watching you like hawks, and copying what they see Mum and Dad doing with a fiendish accuracy! So make your home a place where everything is in harmony with Jesus' love. Let it not be a place where carping criticism is in the air, and strict puritanism rules, but where the warmth of true Christian character lives.

You'll remember that Jesus gave us only one commandment, and that was to love. 'As I have loved you — so love one another.'

So I pray that Jesus may work his miracle in your lives starting from today. May he take what you now are, and over the years of sharing that you do, expand your love and warmth, compassion and generosity. May he be so richly in your new home that he may be able, as I am sure that he wishes, to take the ordinary loaves and fishes of your daily living and bless them into a banquet for you and everyone who knows you.

May God bless you both.

18
WEDDING
PATTERN-MAKING

Some people get a bit 'up tight' and cynical about the wedding customs we have in England. Most couples, I guess, in the days leading up to their wedding, look at all the things that have to be done and threaten to elope to get away from them. I can understand that feeling very well, because on the face of it they're all very silly.

Let's imagine what a little man from Mars would think if he were sitting on the church doorstep at a wedding. Consider it. First he'd see a couple of gentlemen arrive dressed up to the nines in clothes they don't normally wear, looking acutely uncomfortable. Then a group of pretty ladies arrive wearing dresses that can never be used again, even at parties. A crowd of people arrive, the ladies wearing hats that blow off in the wind, and which they hardly ever wear either. Then a special car arrives, and it's so special that you'd never be able to take it shopping, or park it in a supermarket car park. Out of it gets a lady in a beautiful white dress that costs the earth and that she'll never wear again, perhaps with a veil over her face so that people don't know who she is, except that it's so thin that everyone *can* tell who she is. And then after about 45 minutes, everyone comes out of church and they throw little bits of coloured paper all over each other. Well! This little man from Mars would think that the people who live on this planet were all harmlessly dotty.

And, let's face it — he'd be right! These things we do on wedding days *are* a bit nonsensical. But I'm not supercilious about them. Why not? Because we are all human — we are pattern-making animals.

When we feel deeply about something we have the built-in need to DO something and not just talk about it. When we want to express something very profound, words aren't enough. For example, if we've had an argument with somebody at work and want to have a fresh start, what do we do? We buy them a drink, or shake their hand, don't we? The words, 'let's forget it' aren't enough. If we want to tell a child that we love it we don't just say so, we pick it up and give it a cuddle don't we? We're made that way. When there's trouble in our relationships, we 'kiss and make up.' We're pattern-making people.

Of course, in church we know all about this, because of what we describe as sacraments — outward and visible signs of deep inward truths — the water when we baptize a baby, the bread and wine when we express our loyalty to Jesus our founder. We handle the same things as He did. These are actions that we *do*, not just things that we say.

So the same thing applies to your wedding today. It's a unique day for you both, and you're celebrating a unique relationship. You want, naturally enough, to express this in as satisfying a way as you can. What's happening today, your commitment to each other, is too profound for words. You can't express what you feel in language, which you may or may not remember in the days ahead. You have the instinctive need to underline it in actions. So the central part of your wedding today has been two actions.

1. YOU JOINED HANDS

This symbolized colleagueship, partnership. It means that whatever life may throw at you, you'll face it together, you'll deal with as a couple. It involves finding a solidarity between you, so that when life tries to get at you it'll find it's up against not one vulnerable person, but a strong union of two. Chesterton once said, 'Marriage is an armed alliance against the outside world.' That's very true.

This will make demands on you, physically, emotionally, and spiritually, but the success of your marriage will depend on how well you can respond to those demands. It isn't marriage that fails — it's people who fail. The challenge is how to turn that joining of hands into a lifelong partnership — how to turn two into one.

I heard of a rather sloppy fellow whose friend looked at his jacket, and saw that all the buttons were firmly sewn on. 'Ah I can see you're married now,' he said. 'Oh yes,' said his friend, 'that's the first thing she did — taught me how to sew them on.' Colleagueship.

2. YOU EXCHANGED WEDDING RINGS

This is an old custom which symbolizes that your relationship, like your rings, has no end. It's a relationship that goes on throughout life, continuing as the years pass. Your love for each other should have no stop or start.

Your rings, however, do have an inside and an outside. So will your marriage. It will have its private emotional content — its inner battles — its victories and defeats. It will also have its public face which will be seen by relatives, friends, and the outside world. Your rings symbolize all of that.

Sometimes these rings will get in the way. Sometimes they'll be worn with pride. Sometimes they'll be shining bright. At other times they'll be covered with paint or dirt. Sometimes, in the case of the bridegroom at least, they'll be regularly washed with dish-water. But covered with suds or not, those rings will always be there, reminding you of the deep commitment you have made to work for each other's good — however the years pass.

So you'll take away with you today material things which

will bring back memories in years to come. The Wedding Certificate, the photographs, ornaments off the wedding cake, your rings — memories of things worn, and actions done. Our wish for you is that you'll look at these things in the years ahead with fondness, and that all the silly wedding customs we inflict on ourselves will be remembered with affection because of what they mean, and the deep relationship that they express.

When you cut the cake, your first joint action as a married couple, may it be the first of a long series of happy things you do together. May your experience of life be as varied and rich as the cake itself. May you never choke on the hard bits, and may your relationship be as sweet as the icing.

God bless you both.

19

WEDDING

LIGHT AND SHADE

This is, so you are always being told, Your Happiest Day. You have promised yourselves to each other, 'for better for worse, for richer for poorer, in sickness and in health.' That's a mighty deep commitment! But don't be frightened of it because of that. Relatives seem to get a perverse delight in telling you all about the problems of marriage, and making your hair curl with gory stories, don't they?

I heard about an old couple who celebrated their diamond wedding, and relatives were asked how they remained so healthy. 'Well,' they said, 'whenever the dinner isn't fit to eat, instead of losing his temper, Bill goes out into the garden and bangs things about in the shed. Then, whenever he's late home and Mary feels like throwing a pot at him, she goes down to the shops to cool off. They've both lived to this ripe age because they're always out in the fresh air.'

And you know what they say about bridegrooms — a man isn't complete until he's married, then he's *finished*.

But don't you pay attention to all the stories people tell you. Your marriage will be what you make it, and after the tough times you've seen, you deserve all the happiness we could wish you.

When you think of it, all great advances come through struggle. You would think, for example, that from a South Sea island — where life is easy, and there's plenty of time for sitting and thinking, there would come great technological improvements — forward strides in civilization — advances in philosophical thought, but no.

These things have come from people who were caught up in trouble. They are the fruits of battling against high odds, the achievements of struggle. The highest and noblest spiritual qualities we know in Christian civilization come from the life of Jesus who was subject to criticism, apathy, a trumped up criminal charge, and an unjust death. It seems to be a fact of life that the seeds of personal and social good grow best in disturbed and troubled soil, buffeted by strong winds, and watered with tears.

So if, during these past years you've found life difficult, and you've had to bear heavy burdens and be tough, you will find that this is a big plus for you both. Your own experience as individuals will make your marriage stronger, deeper and more satisfying than if life had been a bed of roses.

I once worked in an art gallery selling pictures. I didn't sell many but I learned to appreciate paintings, and the skill of artists in making a one-dimensional picture live. The sense of depth in some of them is tremendous. Your eye is taken deep into landscapes — you seem to be able to walk into them.

There are artistic tricks to that. The main one is to use alternate strips of light and dark. A bright flower in the foreground, a darker leaf behind that, then a brighter curtain behind that, then a dark wall, then a bright window.

It seems so realistic, yet it's all one flat canvas. It's the mixture of light and dark that creates the depth.

And so in your lives and in your marriage. As you walk hand-in-hand into your future you'll walk through light times and dark times — as we all do. Supporting each other, emotionally and physically, your marriage will deepen as a relationship at each change of light. Don't run away from your problems, face them, for these experiences will give your marriage its depth.

Lastly, you know that in the really deep places of life — in birth, in death, in the total commitment of love — we feel a sense of being in the presence of the mysterious. It makes some people wonder, some shiver and some pray. We have a name for this mystery and we call it GOD. Holy and good people ever since Psalm 23 have described him as 'The Good Shepherd', and have come to the conclusion that this meaning, this mystery, is benevolent, personal, and loving, and wants us to be loving too. Christians see the supreme example of this in Jesus, of course.

In the deepest points of your marriage, when your love is as profound as it can ever be, you will feel a sense of that mystery — you will have touched the hand of God.

Jesus went to a marriage feast and helped it along. I think I know him well enough to say he'd be with yours as well, turning the water of an ordinary relationship into something very special.

Later on, people will be standing up and making speeches about you which will be as embarrassing to you as it will be painful to them. There are others in the church today who would run a mile if you even suggested that they make a speech, but their good wishes for you both are just as sincere. So may I say on behalf of all those of your relatives and friends who won't be standing up at the reception — it's our hope and prayer that whatever light and shade may lie before you both in the future, that your marriage will deepen and become even more satisfying with each year that passes.

May God bless you both.

20
WEDDING
THE BEST IS FREE

Weddings are an occasion for a great splurge. Money is no object, and I seem to remember a recent consumer article which reckoned that the average wedding costs something like £10,000. Well, that might be the case in Chelsea or Kensington, round here we're a bit more careful with our brass. Even so, the Bride's father has every right to look a bit sardonic when he's had to give the bride away — 'Give away?' Mind you, in some countries the bride has to have a dowry which bankrupts the family for decades. So, (Bride's father), be thankful about that!

But really, nobody begrudges making it a splendid day for (Groom and Bride), they deserve it, and we're all happy to make sure that it's as good a launch on the sea of matrimony as it can possibly be. The ironic thing, however, is that the things which will make your marriage a happy and successful one have nothing at all to do with money.

FOR INSTANCE, FAITH

From now on you will have faith in each other. You,(Groom), will know, that on days when everything goes wrong, when other people think you're a bent reed, and when you've even begun to lose faith in yourself, there'll be one person at home who'll always think that you're the best thing since sliced bread. She'll bolster your confidence, build up your morale, put a spring in your step, make sure your tie's straight, that your hair's combed, and be quite sure that you can do it — whatever it is.

And the same for (Bride). At times when life gets on top of you, when the problems multiply like greenfly, and you're tempted to give in — you won't, because there'll be one person at home convinced that you'll rise to every challenge. When our younger daughter gave birth to her first child I said, 'Congratulations — I knew you had it in you.'

I did hear of a wife who got it all wrong. The husband had weighed himself at the seaside on one of those 'Tell your fortune' weighing machines. As the card dropped out of the slot the wife picked it up and read it out loud, 'You are a leader with a magnetic personality and a strong character. You are witty, intelligent and attractive to the opposite sex.' The wife then turned the card over, and said, 'It's got your weight wrong as well.'

Have faith in each other — in each other's abilities, character, and attitude. It's an essential part of any good marriage, certainly part of a Christian marriage. For we believe that Jesus has faith in us, and asks us to have faith in him.

> You can't buy that faith. You can't sell it.
> You can't bully or bribe anyone into it.
> You can only give it freely.

HOPE IS ANOTHER OF THOSE QUALITIES

Life, as you know, and if you don't, you'll soon find out, is a succession of little deaths and little resurrections. Every time a door closes it's a grief, and every time a new one opens it's a new life beginning. For your parents your marriage today is a bit of both. There's bereavement in it as well as happiness — that's why all the ladies here have their handbags full of tissues.

The Christian hope is always to see the joy through the sorrow — to see the positive in the negative. So when you, (Groom), can see nothing but black clouds, (Bride) will point out the bright horizon. When you, (Bride), are stuck in the here and now, (Groom) will point you to a sunny tomorrow. That's hope.

You have a right to your personal hopes, and you'll have at least one other person who sees that vision and shares those hopes. For without them, life would be a poor thing. Without lifting our eyes to far prospects, without dreams, without ambitions, even flights of fancy, and castles in the air — without hope, we'd be nothing but earthbound plodders.

As someone once said, 'Some people look at life and see just a hopeless end, the Christian looks and sees an endless hope.' Because when we bring Jesus into the calculation, the sums begin to add up.

> You can't buy hope. You can't sell it,
> You can't bribe or bully anyone into it.
> You can only give it freely.

THE THIRD THING WHICH MONEY CAN'T BUY IS LOVE

Don't confuse it with *'falling in love'*. That's a disease, like a benevolent version of measles, and you can *'fall out of it'* as well. Loving within a stable relationship is a much more permanent, deeper thing. If one can grow from the other, you're all right. If you do, you're in for a long run. I doubt whether love is ever 'at first sight'. It's a slow growing together, and as you share your lives together it deepens and widens.

A little while ago we visited High Force up in the Dales. Like that stream in the hills, your love starts with a waterfall, noisily splashing down the cliff, fizzing and churning, with swift currents going this way and that. It's really quite shallow, but very impressive. But as the river goes on, your love gets smoother and deeper, and though it may not be so demonstrative, the force is actually much more powerful the further it flows down the years.

So you will mingle your love, and it will grow and deepen with each experience you share. It's the heart of your marriage.

> And you can't buy it. You can't sell it.
> You can't bully or bribe it out of each other.
> It can only be given freely.

So, although this will be an expensive day, I can see (*Bride's father*) flinching every time I mention it. It's as well to remember that you can have a wedding as expensive as Elizabeth Taylor's and still not be happy. You can buy a pedigree dog but money can't make its tail wag. You can buy a grand house, but you can't buy a happy home. You can buy a piece of land, but you can't buy peace of mind.

The best things in your marriage, *faith, hope, and love*, are literally priceless. They are at the root of the quality of life that Jesus lived, and asked his followers to live.

If those great virtues can illuminate your home, and generate the sparks between you — you'll be rich indeed.

So I wish you both well, May God's blessing be on your home. May you, (*Bride*), always talk to (*Groom*) in the same way as you answer the phone. And may you find that, like a bottle of wine, (*Groom*) improves with every year that passes.

May God bless you both.

21

WEDDING

HAPPY EVER AFTER

When the Prince saw Snow White lying in a poisoned coma in a clearing in the forest, and couldn't refrain from giving her a kiss — well, they lived happily ever after.

When another handsome Prince finally found the owner of the glass slipper (a most impractical form of footwear I've always thought), the fact that she could hardly walk didn't stop him and Cinderella from living happily ever after either.

That's the thing about fairy stories — they exist in a world where, in spite of wicked aunts and venomous step-mothers, giants and trolls, virtue and innocence always triumph. The bad people get their just deserts and the happy couple set off on their married life in a cloud of pink marshmallow.

Today (*Bride and Groom*), your marriage is a bit like that. There's more than a touch of the fairy story about it. That's why people like weddings. That's why, when you walked up the church drive, all the passers-by stopped, and the customers in the shops opposite glued their noses to the glass — and I've got news for you — they'll be doing it again when you go out!

Make the most of it — make it last as long as possible.

You've entered into your own version of Never Never Land. Enjoy it.

Because, of course, it can't last. In a few days or weeks you'll come down to earth in a gentle glide, or be fetched down with an almighty thud.

And you will, one grey, drizzling, depressing summer morning, sit opposite each other at breakfast. (The critical time in marriage is breakfast.) You'll look at each other pensively, and say to yourselves, 'What have I done?'

That's when your marriage really starts —
when being 'in love' changes to 'loving' —
when feelings have to be translated into effort —
and romance has to be converted into work.

Because there are real dragons, giants and trolls out there, and they'll destroy your marriage given half a chance.

THERE IS, FOR INSTANCE, THE DRAGON OF CYNICISM

There are people who, because their own marriages have failed, find it difficult to accept that your marriage can be happy and succeed.

Don't let them cloud your own relationship. You have today stated that you believe that a life-long relationship between a man and a woman can work, and bring happiness to both. You, (*Groom*), and you, (*Bride*), have been positive that you two can make it work — that you believe in marriage and in each other. Hold on to that come hell and high water. Hold on to it whatever anyone else may say Put salt on that dragon's tail, and tell the cynics to get lost.

THERE IS THE GIANT OF SELFISHNESS

He's lying in wait as well. You are now married, and you can't any longer behave as if you're single. It may seem a simple and obvious point, but the simplest things are sometimes difficult to grasp.

It must always be 'we' and not 'I'. To enjoy things without your partner — that's selfish, and it'll destroy your marriage. To carry your problems by yourself and not share your difficulties — that's equally selfish, and can just as easily destroy your marriage. The old proverb, *a trouble shared is a trouble halved* is very true; it's also true that *a joy shared is a joy doubled.*

The whole point of marriage is to do things together, to share each other's lives, to face the future hand-in-hand — that's what it's all about.

So when you meet the giant of selfishness, slay him quick.

THERE'S THE WITCH OF NON-COMMUNICATION

She's ready to put a spell on you, too. I heard of one old man who was asked whether he had any secrets from his wife. 'Oh yes,' he replied, 'I have £500 in the building society that she doesn't know anything about, and she has £200 tucked away which I don't know anything about.'

Talk to each other. Share not only the facts of what you do, but your feelings, your reactions to each other. It doesn't have to be in words. One of our experts here reckons that only 30% of communication between husband and wife is verbal. There are many ways to communicate — use them all. If you do that the witch's spells won't work on you.

There are many other wicked witches and trolls lining up to threaten your marriage. But I'll let you into the secret of how to see them all off.

If you fight them together, as a partnership, you'll always win. If that love you have between you is a strong bond, and you never let anything or anyone get in between you, you may not win all the battles of life but you'll win your marriage.

If the love you have for each other, which is a small reflection of the love God has for you both, keeps you together whatever happens — then you can set your sights on your Golden Wedding.

So the handsome prince, (*Groom*), has won the heart of the beautiful princess (*Bride*), and you are galloping off into the sunset. May the love of God, of which your rings are a symbol, protect you against all the dragons in your path.

And may he richly bless you both.

22
WEDDING
LIFE'S DRAMA

'All the world's a stage, and all the men and women merely players.'

Well, I suppose so. Someone once said that marriage is a drama in three acts. In Act 1, he talks and she listens, in Act 2, she talks and he listens, and in Act 3, they both talk and the neighbours listen. Well, I don't know about that but certainly there's a drama in life, a story line of mingled comedy and tragedy — laughs and tears. And drama, good drama at least, holds the mirror up to real life, reflects it, and enlarges it.

For instance, in a good play the characters are not just cardboard cut-outs or caricatures, but are real, and have real relationships. And the success of your marriage will depend on your relationship. That's where the true drama of your life is, except that it's real and not make-believe. You'll discover that you won't be able to put on a pretence with your partner, you can't hide behind the grease paint, you've got to be real. There's an old-fashioned word called *integrity* that's at the heart of your relationship. You will be, because you have to be, absolutely straight with each other. Your relationship has to be an honest relationship, where you can genuinely be yourself, and are welcomed and loved for what you really are. It's having just one other person who knows what you are really like, and loves you anyway.

In marriage, success doesn't depend on money, attractiveness, good jobs, or a nice house — that all helps but its really only the scenery; its your relationship that's centrestage, and it's on this that the success of the whole thing turns. If it goes wrong, the whole thing collapses. I heard of one marriage that ended because of incompatibility. His income, and her 'patability'. Rubbish! It's when the relationship breaks down that the marriage falls apart.

Hard times can be coped with if you face them together. Good times can be even more enjoyable if they are generously shared between you both. It's the hope and prayer of all of us here today that your marriage will not just be an outward show, but the visible sign of a deep and vibrant relationship between you both.

As the play goes on the relationship between the characters develops as they act and react with each other.

This is a reflection of real life too, and particularly of marriage. You are both marrying one very complicated person. There's a rumour floating around Ireland, I understand, that the church is authorizing each husband to have 16 wives. 'Four better, four worse, four richer, and four poorer.'

There is in fact just one of each of you, but you may well have 16 sides to your personality, and your partner is just as intriguing. So all your life you'll be building and developing the relationship between you. In action and reaction, in agreement and in tension, month by month, year by year, that relationship will deepen.

It's our wish, all of us here today, that you'll take the principle of love that St Paul talked about earlier in the service and work it out between you. It's the heart of what Jesus lived and died for, and the basis of quality Christian living. May the working out of it between you be a joy both to you, and to all those who love you.

A good play, to be successful, has to be worked at. The scenery has to be constructed, the lights, the sound, the lines and music have to be learned, the movements co-ordinated. Hours, weeks, months of work.

It's just the same in a marriage. Good marriages don't just happen. And largely it's a matter of changing yourself rather than your partner. In marriage *being* the right person is just as important as *marrying* the right person.

I heard of one bride who was very nervous at the wedding rehearsal. The vicar emphasized that the first thing was to come up the AISLE, secondly, go to the ALTAR, then, thirdly, sing a HYMN. 'Remember that,' he said. When the day came she processed up the aisle muttering all the way, 'AISLE, ALTAR, HYMN — AISLE, ALTAR, HYMN.' When she got to the front the bridegroom had gone!

Working at a marriage means working on yourself rather than each other. Don't try to change each other, change yourselves. You will both become better individuals because of the adjustments you make to how you see things and do things.

And so you have all the good wishes of your friends and relatives here — that, as the drama of your marriage unfolds to include dramatic scenes, comic scenes, and tragic scenes, it will succeed and be abundantly satisfying because of the teamwork that you both put into it.

May God's grace rest richly upon you both as the curtain goes up. May you look back on today as the greatest première of your lives.

May you, (*Groom*), always play the romantic lead, and may you, (*Bride*), know that for one person at least you are always the leading lady. May God bless you both.

23

WEDDING

THE BOND

There's plenty of jargon about these days, and social workers are as prone to it as anybody. When they discuss families they talk about 'bonding' — the bonding of husband and wife, the bonding of children to the parents.

Well, I'm afraid I have a simple mind, and being an enthusiastic but not very competent 'Do-It-Yourself-er', I thought 'bonding' was all about glue and sticking things together.

And come to think of it, that's what I've done to you, (*Bride and Groom*), today, isn't it. I've *bonded* you together. It's as if just before you joined hands I'd put a smear of glue between you. To put it another way — you're 'stuck' with each other. How stuck is the question.

Because there are, of course, many kinds of glue.

THERE'S PASTE FOR EXAMPLE

I hope you're not bonded with that. It's water soluble, that's the trouble. It would be a poor marriage that came apart when you put your hands in the sink to do the washing up. Setting up house together is a wonderfully exciting thing.

Marriage is like a game of poker — you start off holding a hand and end up with a Full House. But, however humble it may be, you can express yourselves, and do it up as you wish. If you want purple carpets and pink ceilings, go ahead. Just don't expect to sell it afterwards.

And I can assure you of this, however long you live there, it'll never be finished, there'll always be jobs you want to do. What you're doing is nest-building, and it'll keep you happily occupied for all of your lives. And it's got to be a joint thing that you do together. If the glue that bonds you together comes unstuck with water, or turps, or wallpaper paste, then there's something wrong. Throw yourselves into your home-building and make it a joint enterprise.

In America they don't like the term 'housewife'. Ask a lady what she does and, if she hasn't got a job, she says she's a 'home-maker'. I like it. The only query I have is that it's a man's job too. You must both make sure that the bond you have isn't weakened but strengthened by the process of making your home together.

ANOTHER SORT OF GLUE IS THE STUFF YOU PUT IN A GLUE GUN, OR IRON ON

Its tough stuff used in the right way, but the trouble with it is that it gives way when it gets hot. Don't let your marriage bond get like that. There will be times in your lives, as there are in everyone's marriage, when the heat is on, and trouble comes.

When our children got married they took with them most of the junk they'd accumulated down the years, including the teddy bears they had when they were children. Have you taken yours? Well, if you have, you need to give them new names. Call them Bear and Forebear. Because that's what you'll have to do when the difficulties start to pile up. They're essentials in every home worth its name. Sometimes in life you just have to grit your teeth and battle on until things get better. Sometimes you'll think that things will *never* get better, so put Bear on the mantelpiece and soldier on.

Sometimes your difficulties will be with each other. Neither of you is perfect, and 'gearing-in' to each other may not be very easy after the first blissful novelty. You're both old enough to have developed your own ways of doing things, and you're going to have to adjust them to fit. Sometimes you won't mind, at other times you will, and you'll have to talk it over and compromise. When that happens get the other teddy out — Forebear, and put him on the mantelpiece until you've sorted it out. Actually, when you look at the stories of Jesus in the New Testament you realize just how much he kept hammering at the importance of keeping going to the end, forebearance. So stick at it, and I hope your marriage won't be like the heated glue, where the bond parts when times get hot.

THEN OF COURSE, YOU COULD BE BONDED WITH SUPERGLUE

It seems like very watery and weak stuff when you squeeze it out of the tube, but when the bits have been held together for a few minutes, it's impossible to break. It's the 'Jesus' factor, because his love had that quality. Make your marriage bond like that, even in the uncertain world of today. *Especially* in the uncertain world of today.

Tensions may come of kinds you cannot yet imagine — don't let them break your bond. Pressures may be on you, either both or individually — don't let them snap you apart. Stresses may threaten your relationship — don't let them fracture the love you have.

Hold on to each other whatever may come. May your love be strong enough, and flexible enough, to cope with anything. May your affection for each other be such that no-one and nothing will be able to get between you. It's marvellous what a quick cuddle in the airing cupboard will do for a marriage. And if it's any encouragement, (Bride), the nutritionists say that every kiss reduces your weight by three calories.

So may your union be filled with respect for each other, liking for each other, and love for each other. May your bond be unbroken until the end of your lives . . . and may God bless you both.

24

WEDDING

LIFE AND DEATH

The other day I heard of a bride who was being driven in a taxi to the church for her wedding. Half-way there she thought of something, and leaned forward and tapped the taxi-driver on the shoulder. The man hit the roof, and the taxi squealed to a skidding halt in the middle of the road. Then the taxi-driver turned round and with a dead white face said, 'I'm sorry love, but I usually drive the hearse.'

Now there's a truth in there somewhere if we can unpack it. There's an element of old things ending about today as well as new things beginning. There are chapters of life closing, as well as new chapters opening. There's the feature of the birth and the funeral in your wedding today.

FOR INSTANCE, YOUR RELATIONSHIPS WILL CHANGE

The old comfort to parents is to say, 'You haven't lost a daughter, you've gained a bathroom,' but that has a poignant edge to it, too. When children leave home to get married, the house seems awfully quiet without them. One of our church members recently had the wedding of his fourth and last daughter. He complained bitterly that all these years he'd been able to sit in the corner minding his own business while the women nattered — but now he's having to talk to his wife again! When sons and daughters leave home, parents miss them, and the better the relationship has been the more you miss them.

Sensible parents realize that they *must* withdraw into the background. For if the couple are to make a success of their marriage, their first whole-hearted commitment must be to each other. Neither must feel that their partner's love or loyalty is at all split. The parents' role is to retire into a different function, supporting, encouraging, welcoming, but never interfering or demanding.

So some parts of your old relationships will have to change, some aspects dying down to allow other aspects to grow. There must be the hint of the funeral there as well as the baptism.

Your new relationship is your growth point. Your partner must be the first person to share your news and little secrets with. You must sort things out between you and put up a united front before you share them with anyone else. A writer once said:

> In an ideal marriage husband and wife are loyal to each other not because it is their duty but because it is their joy.

From that consultation and agreement, from that love and loyalty, your relationship will develop, and you will learn from experience that you can totally trust each other. So a new and great relationship is born.

YOUR WEDDING ALSO INVOLVES THE FUNERAL OF YOUR SINGLENESS

The biggest way you'll notice this is in your leisure time. If you're going to find time to spend with each other, and time to visit the expanded circle of relations you've now got, some things will have to go. And it won't always be easy to find a fair and workable compromise. Inevitably, some activities will have to die so that others may be born.

If you work in the evenings, as ministers do, it's even worse. I heard of one minister who said, 'I always wondered where my wife went in the evenings; one night I got home early and there she was!' Clearly, you need a balance between togetherness and separateness, and the togetherness has to be properly distributed between socializing with others and having time just with each other. Now there's no set formula for this, so you must find it for yourselves. But some activities will have to be put aside to make it happen.

THERE'S ANOTHER ASPECT TO THE DEATH OF YOUR SINGLENESS

Because you can't any longer be responsible just for yourself. Your responsibilities have grown by what you have done today.

You are responsible to and for each other, for a start. I don't just mean bills, and legal things, but emotional burdens. When your partner's weighed down with troubles and worries, they'll be your troubles and worries too.

You'll also have added responsibilities in the community, because your new family is one of the building blocks of society — a nursery of what makes a place worth living in. And I believe, as a Christian, that we have responsibilities to God to create in our families such a radiant core of loving living, that they'll influence not just our neighbours, but generations yet unborn.

It's the birth of these new and wider responsibilities that will take the place of the lesser responsibility that has died.

And that's the heart of it really — a love that is creative, deep and lasting; a love that works out the love we see in the life of Jesus and in the rest of the New Testament. If you'll take my advice — don't go looking for happiness, for if you search for it you'll never find it. Just love unselfishly without expecting a return, and it comes back to you bringing happiness with it. For love demands a response. You cannot be loved and not react. The exchange of love is the heart of your relationship, and it's especially important that you both recognize it in the first five crucial years. May your love, which is a human reflection of God's love, be at the heart of your home and your relationship in the years to come.

There's a wonderful sentence in Paul's second letter to Timothy in the Bible:

For God has not given us the spirit of fear;
but of power, and of love, and of a sound mind.

What a combination! Power, love and a sound mind. With a marriage like that, you can go anywhere, do anything, find great fulfilment and happiness, and have the time of your lives, all your lives.

We all wish it for you both. You'll have your births and deaths, like the rest of us. You'll have to recast and reconstitute your lives several times, as we all do. But we pray that because of the power of your togetherness, the love you have for each other, and the sound mind that comes from your joint decisions, you'll find great satisfaction and joy in the years ahead.

May God bless you both.

25
WEDDING
SOMETHING OLD,
SOMETHING NEW...

My first words must be words of congratulation to both of you. Your families, friends and I wish for you all that you wish for yourselves. I recall the young church lady who was warned by the minister not to make her prayers selfish. So that night she prayed, 'Lord, I'm not asking for myself, but please give mother a new son-in-law.' Well, all the planning and hoping has come to its fulfilment today — your mother, (Bride), has got a new son-in-law, and I'm sure that both lots of parents are delighted with both of you, and hope you'll be very happy.

There's a tradition that on her wedding day, the Bride wears something old, something new, something borrowed, something blue.

SOMETHING OLD

Well, you can't get much older than marriage itself. The institution must be, formally or informally, as old as humanity. There's something in us that wants and needs permanent and secure bonding between man and woman. It's how we're made, most of us, physically and emotionally.

The community is made up of family units, where

responsibilities can be shouldered, joys spread wider, and children can be brought up surrounded by care and love. Yes, it's an old institution, but none the worse for that.

I remember having a discussion with a television producer in the BBC canteen in London — he was making a programme about 'The End of Marriage.' 'News to me,' I said, 'Where do you live?' 'South Kensington,' he replied. 'Ah, well,' I nodded wisely, 'that explains it.' Marriage hasn't died in our area — in the real world. And I don't think it's going to die either. It's somehow built-in to how the Creator made the world, and how he made us.

The forms of ceremony may change down the generations — the customs, the white dress, the flowers, the uncomfortable suits hired from Moss Bros, the Best Man's duty to embarrass the Bridegroom at the reception — all these things are traditional. Like the Bride's mother with her handbag full of handkerchiefs. The Bible doesn't say so, but I reckon that's what Eve did when her daughter got married.

So if you want something old, there's nothing more hallowed by time, by human nature, and by God — than a man and a woman, falling in love, and marrying each other. And long may it continue.

SOMETHING NEW

Well, we won't have to look very far for that today. You're wearing all sorts of new things. Indeed, (Bridegroom's) parents have probably insisted that he ditch his own jeans and sweater and kit himself out properly. Parents are like that.

And, of course, there's all the new wedding presents to open and play with when you get the time, 'A*nother* toast-rack, just what we needed!'

But the real newness is in the family unit you've today laid the foundation of. It's a physical, emotional, and spiritual bonding that is quite unique to you. I've heard marriage described as like eating a Chinese meal with chopsticks — it looks easy until you try it. In my young days I rode a motor bike. When my wife was on the back we had to find our balance. We both had to learn to sway the same way and to the same degree going round corners. The first time we tried, we nearly went through the glass front doors of a cinema. Well, being married is a bit like that. As you gear your lives together, make your compromises, and find your joint balance it'll be something entirely new for both of you — and quite unique to you.

May this discovery be not a pain, but a delight for you both.

SOMETHING BORROWED

What you have borrowed today is something that is a great treasure. You come here, not like chicks newly hatched, but from homes where you have been valued and loved, schools where you have been taught. I'm sure you'd want today to pay your tribute and express your gratitude to those who have done the caring and the teaching and the loving down the years. The standards you have now, and will apply to your marriage in the future, are those in which you have been reared — they're borrowed. I hope they've been good Christian standards, based on what you know of Jesus and of his teaching. Keep them, improve on them if you can, and hand them on to your children. May they in future years thank God for the home in which they were brought up.

SOMETHING BLUE

Well, the blue could stand for lots of things. But let it signify today the blue skies that we hope you'll enjoy together. Only a fool would wish you continual pleasure. That's unrealistic, and anyway, sunshine all the time creates deserts, doesn't it? But may there be enough clear blue skies in your marriage to lift your spirits and keep you going.

In fact, though, you can make your own blue skies most of the time. If you tackle your difficulties on the upbeat, if you approach life positively, if you see the best in each other, and in whatever happens, and not the worst, you can paint the sky blue yourselves.

St Paul put it very well in one of his letters:

> If you believe in goodness, and if you value the approval of God, fix your minds on whatever is true and honourable, and just and pure, and lovely and admirable...then the God of peace will be with you.

God bless you both.

26
WEDDING
FOUNDATIONS

You're looking very pretty today, (Bride). Well, I should hope so after all the trouble you've taken over your appearance — it's been worth the effort.

Now I'm no expert on ladies make-up. I only know what I read in women's magazines in the dentist's waiting room, and see in TV adverts. But I gather that putting your face on is quite a complicated system. First you need foundation cream, then you plaster on the layers one by one. The point I'm making is that the foundation has got to be right, otherwise it looks horrible.

Now (Bridegroom), you'll find this principle is true for you, if you don't already know it. You'll be given a wallpaper roll or a paintbrush, and told to get on with it. And you'll be aware that you can't just slap it on — the surfaces have to be prepared first. The old paper has got to be got off, and the old paint smoothed down and sanded. It's got to look a lot worse before you can make it look better. It's a matter of getting the foundation right.

What I want to say today is that your marriage and your family life are just the same. The foundation of it is all-important.

SOME PEOPLE THINK THE BEST FOUNDATION FOR A HAPPY MARRIAGE IS MONEY

If only . . . we came up on the National Lottery, if only . . . we suddenly came into a few thousand, we'd be happy. You wouldn't. You'd have the choice of which misery you prefer, but you wouldn't be happy. If money was a good basis for marriage you'd expect that millionaires and industrial tycoons would have the best marriages of all. But they don't, not by a long chalk! You'll have to work and earn in order to keep going, and I hope you'll have enough to jog along comfortably. But don't go overboard on it. The single-minded pursuit of money costs too much, and one of the prices you pay is your marriage.

SOME PEOPLE THINK THAT THE BEST FOUNDATION FOR A HAPPY MARRIAGE IS GOOD LOOKS

Well, everyone wants their partner to be attractive. There was a great Church leader of the last century, C H Spurgeon, who advised young ministers to marry women full of grace and beauty — so that when they fell from grace they could still live with them.

But if physical attraction by itself is the only thing that keeps you together, your relationship won't last a year. If beauty was a good foundation for marriage you'd expect that film stars and fashion models would have the best marriages of all. But they don't, not by a long chalk. By all means, take trouble over your appearance, for your own sake, and each other's — but don't give it undue importance. It's a fragile foundation.

THE BEST FOUNDATION FOR A HAPPY MARRIAGE THAT I KNOW OF IS THE KIND OF LOVE THAT PAUL TALKED ABOUT IN OUR READING (1 Corinthians 13)

It's a love that is rich in the human resources you pour into it — a love that has a wealth of generosity between you, and I don't just mean bunches of flowers and boxes of chocolates, but generosity of judgement — a love that is full of forgiving and thanksgiving — a love that's overflowing with concern and care. Now those are the values which Paul talks about, and which we see in the life of Jesus which is at the heart of Christian belief — those are the things which *do* make a happy marriage.

And they make the kind of relationship that's really rich and beautiful. You know, as I do, that sometimes you can go into a house which has had a fortune spent on it, it has all the latest and best stuff. And yet, there's an *edgy* feel to the place. Brittle, uncomfortable — it's a house but not a home. Yet, in other houses, where the furnishings are not as nice, the sofa's worn, and the wood isn't as polished, and it's a bit untidy — you get the feeling that the people there have built up something between them. There's a tone, an atmosphere, a rich beauty in there somewhere between them. Now that's the quality which *does* make a happy marriage.

So it all depends on the foundation, doesn't it? Any regular churchgoers here will remember one of the stories that Jesus told. He talked about house foundations. Well, he knew what he was talking about; after all, he worked as a jobbing builder. He talked about a house built on sand which collapsed when the wind blew and the flood waters rose. He also talked about a house built on rock, which withstood everything thrown at it.

My wish and hope for both of you, and the wish of all your friends and relatives here today, is that your marriage will be surely and soundly based on good foundations. That the relationship between you will be of such a strong and secure love, that whatever the future years will bring, you will stand proud as an example of what a good and happy marriage can be, and create a home that the children will be glad to come from, and others will be glad to go to.

May God bless you both.

27

WEDDING

BEING LOVED

Today, you set the seal on a courtship and relationship that had grown steadily in the past, and now I trust will go on to become fuller and richer. And it's lovely! This is why people have had a good look as the bridal car passed them in the street; this is why they waited at the bottom of the church drive to see you come in. It's more than curiosity. There's something about a wedding that's positive, life-affirming, creative, and it makes people say, '*aaah*'.

Mind you, I did hear a rumour that there's a middle-aged lady in this area who wants to get remarried here, because she's noticed that all the brides go in with an old fellow, and come out with a young one. But apart from her, everyone else is drawn to the central point that you love one another, and that's as it should be.

Psychologists say that the problem with many people these days is that they are 'love starved.' Mother Theresa is quoted as saying, 'The biggest disease today, isn't leprosy or tuberculosis, but rather the feeling of being unwanted, uncared for, and deserted by everybody.' From this service onwards you *belong* to each other. You willingly, lovingly, *belong*. So my wish is that this sense of belonging will grow ever more strongly as the years pass.

When I think of children brought up without affection, security, and a sense of being accepted and loved, I worry about the next generation. But I'd like to turn the coin over and look at the other side of the subject. A real part of this problem is that so many people are not willing or able to *be* loved. Through fear, shyness, hurt, snobbishness, or whatever, they are not psychologically healthy enough to open up to someone else's love. They do not love, and are not loved, because they will not let love in. What a shame!

You are both committed now to loving one another, but also to the more passive and yet more difficult role of allowing yourselves to be loved. This means that you must be open to each other, so that your partner can be open to you. Only in such an atmosphere can real love grow.

Many animals in their courtship rituals adopt a vulnerable position. The albatross, for example, raises one wing to leave himself open to attack. He is, in fact, saying to the future Mrs Albatross, 'I trust you, and I show you, at great risk to myself, that I genuinely trust you.' Loving is a risk, indeed all relationships are risky. In loving each other, and in allowing yourselves to be loved, you are saying to each other, 'I trust you, with what I am now, and with what the rest of my life will hold. I leave myself vulnerable, physically, mentally and spiritually, to you.'

I heard of an inscription on a stone set up in North Africa which reads, 'I, the captain of a Legion of Rome, have learned and pondered this truth, that there are in life just two things, love and power, and no-one can have both.' You have opted for love, and what a tremendous thing to do. It's a noble act of faith in each other. It's what makes weddings such heart-warming occasions — that you can do this.

Now when we set this against the faith of a church like this one, we can see how closely it fits in with what will be preached here tomorrow and every Sunday. We talk and think about a person who lived a life of sacrificial love so thoroughly and profoundly that in the end he gave his life out of love. In the teaching and the example of Jesus we get a wonderful example of what this kind of love is all about.

I don't know whether you've got a collection of 'How to make a Happy Marriage' books. Some of them are all right, but I have my doubts about some of the advice in the marriage books on my shelves. 'Give her some underwear so exotic that she hides it in the bottom drawer,' says one book. 'Don't criticize the housework at tea-time if you want to make love to her that night,' says another. 'Consult the wife before you buy an exercise bike.' Well, yes I suppose so. But a very good book for you to start your family library would be a New Testament, preferably a modern version. Look at the kind of love it talks about, think about how it worked in the life of Jesus, examine the ways it describes that love operating, not just between yourselves, but in a wider context. Ponder over the ways love challenges you to be vulnerable, and consider the way that love is always creative.

Then you'll get the picture, not of the two of you in an isolated relationship, wrapped up in each other, but of a greater cosmic principle in which your love fits — an historical theme of which your relationship is your own personal variation. You'll get a vision of the love of God of which your love is a part.

'Love Divine, all loves excelling,
Joy of heaven to earth come down,
fix in *us* thy humble dwelling,
All thy faithful mercies crown.

My wish for you, and my prayer for you, is that you'll find depths in your relationship like that, and that as a consequence your marriage will be deep, rich and very happy.

May you, (Bridegroom), find that (Bride) is a splendid cuckoo. I mean by this that she'll be able to cook as well as coo. And may you, (Bride), find that (Bridegroom) has discovered the best way to compliment you — that is, frequently.

God bless you both.

28

WEDDING

THE MARRIAGE GARDEN

As you came up the drive into the church today, you passed by the church garden. I hope that you have been conscious enough of your surroundings to notice the flowers and enjoy them. I hope so, because I'm the one who looks after them. I enjoy gardening, and I also think it's important. It's our church's front window, and I hope it implies that it is a colourful, varied, productive and interesting group of people who come here — which it is.

The bluebells, the London pride, the aubrietia, the rhododendrons, and in a few weeks the dahlias and roses, are there because they have benefited from a few basic things that every gardener is aware of, warmth, food, water, and care. Just like a marriage and a home — your home. And where does a home start? With a boy and a girl falling in love. As Winston Churchill once said, 'no superior alternative has yet been discovered.' As a start that's fine, but you, too, will need to cultivate your marriage as I look after the church garden.

YOUR MARRIAGE WILL NEED WARMTH

You'll be building up your home. Getting a house is one thing, creating a home is something else. I heard of a little boy whose parents were having to live in a bed and breakfast. His school-teacher once, in a clueless moment, described him as 'homeless'. 'I'm not homeless, Miss,' he replied, 'We've got a home, we just haven't got a house to put it in.'

Home is a place of peace. A shelter from doubt and division, where one can love, trust, and be vulnerable in safety. Whether it's a hotel room and a suitcase, a bed-sitter, or a splendid desirable residence — your home is a sacred place. It's an oasis of love and respect where the hostile world can be kept at bay, where cynicism and anxiety are locked out, and where fine virtues can flourish.

'We need not power or splendour,
Wide hall or lordly dome;
The good, the true, the tender —
These form the wealth of home.

Who knows what travels you'll be forced to make in the years ahead? What cities, even what countries you might be working in? Who knows where you'll be living? Wherever you may be, keep the ideal of your home, put a high priority on its quality. Whatever it is, fill it with emotional and spiritual warmth. If it's only a suitcase, get a sticker which says 'God Bless Our Home' and stick it inside the lid. Just like the flowers outside, that warmth will make your marriage blossom.

FEED AND WATER YOUR MARRIAGE, AS I DO THE PLANTS

Good gardens don't happen by accident, neither do good marriages. They are made by the love, work and sacrifices of husband and wife.

The little acts of consideration, the sideways glances of

understanding, the giggle of private laughter and sharing your last Jammy Dodger — each of these things is a few drops of water on the seedling of your marriage, helping it to grow and flourish.

Each job done purely to please each other, each present carefully chosen, each tentative hope trustingly shared, each effort to try to understand, each prayer which both of you say — is a drop of fertilizer to help your partnership grow sturdy and strong. Work on your marriage, water it, feed it, then it'll grow healthy and long.

TEND AND CULTIVATE YOUR MARRIAGE

That's what I do in the church garden. There are plants which have to be 'dead-headed', the old blooms have to be removed so that new ones can grow — shrubs that need old wood removed to encourage new flowering shoots. A marriage can be full of dead flowers and old wood too. Your partnership can in the years ahead become too static, too full of stale things. We all need change, development, stimulation. Otherwise a dynamic partnership can become a boring habit. Like the schoolboy howler which read, 'One husband married to one wife is called monotony.'

There are the pests to keep away too. Both in the garden and in a marriage. You'll need to tackle them when you see them. I go out late at night with a torch, a shovel and a plastic pot and collect slugs. People going home from the pub see the flashing torch and wonder what I'm up to. Often I hear them say to each other, 'Don't ask!'

The slugs of selfishness and taking each other for granted will gnaw away at your marriage unless you tackle them all the time. The greenfly of not sharing what you think, of not communicating, will eat up your trust in each other. The blight of trying to carry your problems by yourself will kill all the beauty which should be between you.

The battle against these marriage pests is a never-ending war. Keep at it, don't let them get the upper hand. A successful marriage, like a lovely garden, has to be tended continuously.

As you leave the church today, you'll have some photographs taken outside. You'll be in the front of the pictures, and that's as it should be. And we hope that you'll look back on them in fifty years with great nostalgia and happiness.

But in the background, with any luck, there'll be some of the flowers in the church garden. I hope that, flowering in the spring warmth, fed, watered and tended by me, they'll not only enhance your photo album, but also say something significant about your relationship — that they'll be a parable of what your marriage will become.

May God bless your marriage and may the sunshine of his love help it to blossom beautifully in the years to come.

29
WEDDING
THE THINGS YOU'VE BROUGHT

My first words must be ones of congratulations to you both, it's my wish, and that of all your families and friends gathered here today, that your marriage will be all that you hope it will.

You're bound though, (B*ridegroom*), to feel a bit nervous and disorientated. You're stuck at the front, dressed in the uncomfortable Bridegroom's Uniform, with nothing to hold on to but the Best Man. Nice chap though he is — he's really got his mind on what he's going to say at the reception. You, (B*ride*), you've got more people to hold you up, but they're probably more nervous than you are. You've left all your props at home, and you're here, just yourselves. But in fact you've brought a great deal of baggage with you, unseen belongings.

YOU BRING, FOR INSTANCE, YOUR PAST

All the things that have happened to you since you were babies have made you what you are. Your upbringing, your parents' relationship to each other and to you, the brothers and sisters you have, your school, your church, your friendships, your work, all these and a hundred other factors have gone into making you *you*.

You may have clung consciously to the values your parents taught you, or just absorbed them in the process of growing up, and you may value them as your own, and want to thank your parents today for what they did. You may have thought them out carefully and decided for yourself that they're right values and truths worth living by. I hope they're Christian values that won't let you down in the years ahead.

On the other hand, you may have reacted against them, and found different values for yourselves. Perhaps you have explored and discovered for yourselves your answers to the big questions, like, 'Where did we come from? Why are we here? and, Where are we going?' Or maybe you've put those questions on the back burner, as they say, and don't know.

That past — those memories, good or bad, won't go away. You're stuck with them — you're both stuck with them. So share the good memories, let your partner enjoy them with you. Share your bad memories too. Unhealed wounds don't go away, they need careful and gentle healing. Left to fester they will harm your relationship, and the new family you're creating today. Maybe in the next few weeks you'll get your past into true perspective for once. You can afford to be honest with yourself and each other. Grudges and resentments can be shed, forgiveness given and received, and you can find a shared joy and a shared healing.

You have not only given to each other your promises and a wedding ring today, you've also given your past.

YOU ALSO BRING WHAT YOU ARE NOW

You're both young attractive people, deeply in love with each other. Enjoy each other, celebrate each other, revel in each other, delight in each other! And may God bless every moment of your love and your sharing.

The old parody of the Church looking down to see who's enjoying themselves so we can tell them to stop it, is a gross libel.

I heard of a dour Scottish minister. One of his members asked him quietly once, 'Minister, is it right to make love to my wife on the Sabbath?' The minister thought, and said, hesitantly, 'Aye, it is, as long as you don't enjoy it!'

Nonsense! The Bible is full of men and women delighting in each other, in their union and their family. It's how we're made, it's a gift of God — and the New Testament actually uses that powerful symbol as an analogy of Christ the Bridegroom, and his Bride the Church. The physical, mental and spiritual unity of Christ and his followers should be as close and loving as the union between husband and wife.

Your marriage, your love, physical, mental and spiritual, has God's blessing on it — enjoy it. You bring here, and to each other, what you are now.

LASTLY, YOU BRING YOUR FUTURE

We hope there'll be very many years ahead for the both of you.

But that's a double-edged sword, isn't it? It depends on how happy those years will be. The old married hands here today will agree with me that how much happiness you find in your marriage depends on how much happiness you put into it. That happiness you'll have to work out between yourselves as the years pass, and as your relationship deepens and matures in the everyday routine. Marriages may be made in heaven, but they're lived on earth.

You'll get to the point, (Bride), like all Brides, when you stop wondering what to wear, and will ask yourself how long it'll last. And you'll realize, (Bridegroom), that (Bride) will need the help of a stalwart man. She'll need you to hold the steps while she paints the ceiling, for example!

Your future will be a mixture of joys and sorrows I expect, like most of us find — achievements and disappointments.

But may the golden thread of your love for each other run through it all. A great theologian, who wrote massive books, said in the end, after a lifetime of the study of Jesus's life, death and resurrection, that when you sum it all up, 'It is love alone that counts, love alone that triumphs, and love alone that endures.'

Love doesn't have a happy ending, in fact it shouldn't have an ending at all, the Easter component within it brings not happy endings but a succession of new starts. It's the oxygen that keeps your marriage alive. May that love keep you going through all the changes and chances the future may bring for all the years ahead.

With (*Bridegroom*) and (*Bride*) described by occupation on the Marriage Certificate, I could end with some terrible puns on your jobs in my good wishes. But I'll leave that to the Best Man, who's probably thought of them all already. I'll content myself with congratulating you both, and wishing you God's blessing in the years ahead.

30

WEDDING

THE DIFFERENCES

Today's all a bit of a dream isn't it — a lovely pink cloud of fantasy. The prestigious cars, the beautiful dresses held together with strategic safety pins, the flowers carefully matched to the colour of the dresses, the relatives and friends looking more sprucy than you've ever seen them before, the reception where someone else is going to do the washing-up, the toasts — it's a beautiful dream.

Enjoy it, have a good revel while you can. You're old enough and mature enough to enjoy visiting fairyland without wanting to live there. So have fun!

But there are more dangerous fantasies — illusions you may have about each other. Every bride and bridegroom have the preconceived fantasy of marrying the ideal husband or wife. And then slowly reality dawns! And you realize that the person you married isn't absolute perfection. You may be tempted to embark on a reform programme — don't! Only God can make a tree, you know, and it won't work. In any case, any attempt to mould or remake each other to what you personally want — to make them conform to your likes and dislikes — is a bit arrogant and insulting anyway. Your partner was made in God's image, not yours, and they have a right to be different, and to be treated and respected as themselves. You can *allow your partner to change*, but that's their privilege. You can by *compromises and adjustments* gear your lives together as you must, but that's loving adaptation. Both are a long way from manipulating each other's personality or behaviour.

You love each other for what you are now, so accept each other 'as is'. There is a computer term, which computer buffs here today will know, it's called WYSIWYG. It means 'What You See Is What You Get,' the computer screen accurately shows what the printer will produce for you. So, look at each other well, because it's WYSIWYG time. What You See beside you Is What You Get.

There are many recipes for a happy and long lasting marriage. Henry Ford said the secret was the same as making cars — stick to the same model. One wife said that the thing that kept hers together was the notice she put on the television which read 'Danger, excessive watching of football matches damages our marriage.' Another old couple said their idea was to save each other for their retirement. Yet another couple said theirs survived because of good health — they never got sick of each other.

But St Paul was a bit more on the ball when he wrote a letter to some friends. He was on the subject of how to create a happy church, but it's just as good advice for a happy marriage. 'Accept life with humility and patience, making allowances for each other because you love each other.' (Ephesians 4:2)

ACCEPT LIFE WITH HUMILITY AND PATIENCE

The future years will bring what they will bring. There's a randomness about life that's nothing to do with goodness or badness, hard work or laziness. Little offhand actions will produce wonderful results, long worked for schemes will clatter in ruins round your feet. Some years will be good, some reasonable, and some downright disastrous — but that's how life is.

Take each day as it comes, battle through the bad ones, and enjoy the good ones, but do it together, sharing the laughter and the tears. You can 'rage against a blind fate' if you like, but it'll only give you indigestion. Better to take Paul's advice, get through each day together with humility and patience.

We live in a world where everything seems to be reduced to balance sheets. What I suggest is that it would be a good idea if at every Wedding Anniversary you sit round the meal table, look at each other, and any little (*Bridegroom's surname*)s who may join you, and say to yourselves, 'How rich would we be if we lost all our money?' Somehow that question brings everything into a healthier proportion, doesn't it?

MAKE ALLOWANCES FOR EACH OTHER BECAUSE YOU LOVE EACH OTHER

I have talked about not trying to make your partner the same as yourself. The reason is because your differences are important. They matter because your partner's differences hold out the promise of fulfilling your needs.

One of the things that makes people want to get married at all, is the need everyone has to feel *complete*. Consciously or unconsciously that's one of the reasons you have chosen each other. You two will complement each other, and you will both be better, more rounded personalities, more fulfilled individuals *as a result of those differences*.

The trick is, of course, to ignore the differences which harm your relationship, yet enhance the differences that improve it. The only way to do that is to make allowances. And the motive force for that tolerance is the love you have for each other. I've heard love described as, 'an unconditional commitment to an imperfect person.' I couldn't put it any better.

So, take each day as it comes, with humility and patience, and in your love make all the allowances you can. That's Paul. There's no evidence in the Bible, but there's a tradition that Paul was married. I reckon he must have been — he certainly seemed to know what he was talking about.

But that's for another day — you're off to the reception and your honeymoon. Let the blue birds twitter and the confetti fly for as long as it may!

May God bless you both.

31

WEDDING

WATER INTO WINE

If you go to Galilee in Israel, there's a small dusty village called Cana. You'll see a Christian church which is supposed to be built on the place where Jesus performed the miracle of turning the water into wine at a wedding feast.

In the entrance are some jars which, though not the originals, are supposed to be the sort of jars that were used. If, when you come out of the church, you turn right and go down the lane, you reach an little Arab shop which sells Cana wine. They'll offer you a little glass of it. Beware — it's lethal! On a still night you can hear it seething in the bottle!

It was there, so St John's Gospel records, that Jesus did the very first miracle — at a wedding. It's interesting to ask why St John, out of all the things that Jesus did, put this event first. Nothing in St John is there by accident. He obviously thought that it was particularly significant. It meant to him far more than just the turning of one substance into another; it had, and still has, a wider meaning, and one that applies to you, here, on your wedding day.

You are today celebrating your marriage in a church. You needn't have bothered if just getting married was all you were concerned about. You could have popped down to the Register Office, popped in, done the legal bits, and popped out after ten minutes, husband and wife in the eyes of the state. It would have been an ordinary common or garden legal contract.

Your marriage would have started in this matter-of-fact way, and would probably have gone on like that too. That's the relationship that most husbands and wives are in. Some are happily married, some rather miserably married, and most are just ordinary. And I'm not decrying that, you can't live on a 'high' all the time.

There's a Russian proverb which says, 'Don't praise marriage on the third day, but after the third year.' Let's face it, all marriages are happy, it's living together afterwards that causes all the trouble.

But you want more than that, you have asked for a Christian marriage. You are like the couple in Cana who invited Jesus to come to their wedding, you are inviting him into your home, and into your relationship. That's going to make a difference — as it made a difference to them, so it should to you. The water will be turned into wine, the ordinary will be made something special.

YOUR COMMITMENT TO EACH OTHER IS DEEPER

I heard of an American millionaire who promised the minister a bonus if he made the service as short as possible. It actually went, 'Take him?' 'Yep.' 'Take her?' 'Yep.' 'Took!' But today you've done a lot more than that. You've made a very deep commitment to each other. You've promised to love each other 'for better and worse, richer and poorer, in sickness and in health,' for the rest of your lives.

That's a mighty big thing to promise, it's the deepest commitment any human being can make to another. You may well have to cope with the worse, sickness and poverty — who knows? If you look up *marriage* in an encyclopedia, you'll find it's closely followed by an entry for *martyrdom*.

You have made this loving commitment to each other as you are now, and as you will become in the years ahead. So the water of an ordinary relationship is turned, by your life-long commitment, come what may, into the strong wine of a deep and lasting union.

YOUR PROMISE TO EACH OTHER IS PERMANENT

At a time when so many marriages end in divorce you have promised to love each other as long as you both shall live. You mean this, and are determined to make your marriage work. And you have said this, not just in front of your families and friends, but in this sacred and solemn place, and in the presence of God. That's how seriously you view it. No-one can see what the future holds, or what will happen, but as far as lies in you — this is for keeps.

It's a sobering thought that you have made such an irrevocable step as this, but with it comes a liberty and a security that nothing else can bring. You'll learn as the years pass that you can be sure of each other, you can rely on each other, you can rest easy in that relationship.

So the water of an ordinary promise is turned by God into the comforting wine of a lifelong trust.

YOUR STRENGTH IS INCREASED

In an ordinary marriage, husband and wife rely on their own efforts to face the demands that marriage brings. But today, you have asked for God's help in the coming years. You are recognizing that there's a spiritual dimension to life, to marriage, and in particular to your marriage.

You are open to deep spiritual realities, and this awareness will deepen as a result of your togetherness. You see your love as a 'keying-in' to the profound love of God which is history long and universe wide. If you invite Jesus to work his miracle in your marriage as he did in Cana, this will add a power and a strength to your marriage that nothing else can bring. A good Christian marriage is like a three-legged stool, husband, wife and God, without one of those legs it falls over. So the water of your ordinary love will be turned into the rich wine of a love divine.

So if you ever go to Israel, do visit Cana, and have a little drink of that lethal wine. But whether you do or not, I pray that Christ will work His marriage miracle again between you both as you begin your life together. May an ordinary marriage be turned for you into something very special indeed.

May God bless you both.

32

WEDDING

THE ACCIDENTAL SACRAMENT

Well, here you are, standing in church at long last. After all the months of waiting and preparation, it's actually happening, and I'm sure that you feel that if you pinch yourselves you'll wake up! But no, it's for real, you are genuinely Mr and Mrs (*Groom's surname*).

And I suppose in the next few days you'll be thinking of how you first met, of all the accidental little things that brought you together, and made up the process which have brought you to this great event today. Looking back, it's amazing how those little coincidences have built up.

I heard the story of a cockney lad who had two girl-friends, Kathleen and Maria, and he didn't know which to choose, so he went into a church to pray for guidance. 'When I opened my eyes, there it was,' he said, 'written on the wall — *Ave Maria!* — so I did.'

Most married people remember with affection how we met, the coincidences, the accidental things, the unrelated circumstances that all came together so that we could meet, our friendships develop and ripen into the relationships we have today. There's a bit of the 'Ave Maria', in all of our life stories.

But, and this is the point I want to make today, these

coincidental things can end up as providential things —
they can become what we in the Church call sacramental
things. It's as if they were somehow *meant* to happen. Life's
full of things like that. We in the Church call it the Grace of
God.

The word 'sacrament' means something ordinary which is
irradiated with a deeper meaning and significance. Like the
water at a baby's baptism, like the bread and wine at a com-
munion, like the things that you have done, and will do
today in your wedding. Ordinary things get turned into a
sort of spiritual isotope.

The Roman Catholic Church observes seven sacraments,
and one of them is the sacrament of marriage. Here is an
ordinary situation, a man and a woman come together, a
combination of coincidence, accident, as well as desire.
And the Church says, 'Ah, but there's more to it than that.
God can turn all this coincidental into providential, and
sacramental.' This relationship can develop in the love of
God, into something that is much deeper. He can bless it,
and his love can be reflected between you both. So, say the
Catholics, it's sacramental — and I'll go along with that.

The Quakers, on the other hand, don't identify any particular things as formal sacraments. 'All life is sacramental,'
they say. Every ordinary routine event can reflect the great
eternal realities, if we make it so. And, of course, they are
right as well.

After the excitement of the next few weeks you'll settle
down into a routine. You know what they say. The bride
starts by sinking into his arms, the rest of her life she's got
her arms in the sink.

The looks over supper that are so sweet,
appear a bit different over Shredded Wheat.

But however life fills with routine and ordinary things,
they can be sacraments too, say the Quakers — and they've
got a good point. There are deep bells of togetherness that
ring in our minds and hearts over the washing up, doing the
garden, and all the little loving and caring things we do for

each other in our family circles. To iron a shirt that he will wear speaks very loudly of your love. To mend a kitchen gadget to make life a bit easier for her is a demonstration of your affection.

It's nice to give each other unexpected presents now and again, a favourite meal, a bunch of flowers. But that's extra, your real basic love is demonstrated far more with a screwdriver and an ironing board. All these simple things done for each other become sacramental, because they are done with love and affection. They speak to us of the eternal love of God, which underpins all that we do.

So my good wishes for you are summed up in my wish that your married life may not be just what it seems on the surface. Of course, I hope that the outside appearance, what your family and friends see, will be good and affectionate. But more important, may the inside of your relationship, the quiet moments you have together, be a secret world of rich significance. May you find a deep reservoir of love and trust that will carry you to the profoundest meanings of what life at its best is about.

May your marriage be full of little accidentals that turn into providential blessings, and that, however routine and ordinary life may settle down to be, you'll never lose that divine spark between you.

May God bless you both.

33

WEDDING

COSMIC AND PERSONAL

I expect that you feel very exposed, standing as you do at the front of this church today. There's no way your relatives and friends are going to let you crawl away into a corner, even if you would be very glad if you could. Most of us are happier to sit at the back than stand at the front, and if we're forced to a prominent position, we feel self-conscious and embarrassed. But here you are, dressed up to the nines, taking the central role in all the events of this important day. People will be looking at you, concentrating on you, listening to you, taking photographs of you. What a day!

And in a sense it's important that it should be like this. Because it's a very important day, not just for you, but for your families too. There are big changes that they have to make. There's now a link between two families that wasn't there before. I hope that this link will grow into good friendships as time goes on.

Then their relationship to you will have to change. From today onwards you'll be a brand-new family on your own, and your first loyalty will be to each other. So relatives will be standing back, in a sort of back seat role of encouragement and support.

This new family of yours will be recognized by the community and the country, as a new family unit. You'll be one of the building blocks that make up our society. You'll be a government statistic. You now have an official status, Mr and Mrs (*Groom's name*). But it's more even than that.

Ever since Adam and Eve, men and women have been coming together and creating families in all sorts of formal and informal ways. It's how God made the world and us; it's the pattern of his basic design. And those families have grown and developed the next generation of men and women, who themselves have set up their own families. And so on down the ages. If you can imagine that Adam and Eve were the first link in the chain, every following family has added their link, your parents added theirs, and now you connect your marriage into the chain of families which goes back to the beginning of human life itself.

So your marriage today isn't only important for you, it's important for your families, for society, and it even has a historical significance. I'd like you to see what you've done today not only as the achievement of your own desires, but as a link in God's design for humankind.

But your marriage is a personal affair as well. When you get home, lock the door and draw the curtains, you'll be on your own together. Your relationship is and will be, as it should be, a very personal thing which you will have to work out together. No-one will know the way that you act and react with each other, no-one will be able to help, unless you ask them to. Even then it's doubtful.

We all hope today that this inner core of your relationship will be happy and satisfying in every way, but you'll have to work at it. There are a few things that I can tell you that I'm sure of.

You'll be happier than you've ever been before. You'll have a partner to share your pleasures with, someone to rely on, and share with, a partner to love and be loved by. It's a tremendous experience.

But you'll also be more miserable than you've ever been before. The very love and openness to each other will make you more vulnerable and able to be hurt. Your sorrows are the price tags on your love. You can see the sort of love I mean in the life of Jesus, where his great love had the price tag of a cross. On days when things go wrong, and mis-understanding builds on misunderstanding, when however you try you can't seem to please each other, you'll feel more wretched than you thought possible.

You'll be freer than you've ever been before. There's a liberty that marriage brings, you can do things, and go places as a married couple that you can't as singles. You'll be joining in with other young couples and a new world will open for you both. This brings great possibilities of per-sonal fulfilment. The security of your basic relationship will give you a sound base from which to explore new areas of life.

But you'll also be more restricted than you've ever been before. You'll not be able to do whatever you like with no reference to anyone else; you'll have to think of what your partner wants, and consult them before you decide any-thing. There will be many times when your freedom is restricted because of the demands your new family makes. As the old music-hall song says, 'I can't get away to marry you today, my wife won't let me!'

You'll be more supported and encouraged than you've ever been before. In our teens and twenties we're often very lonely. We have to make personal and private deci-sions on education, careers, jobs, housing, friends, and activities — far-reaching decisions which can affect the rest of our lives. We make these decisions by ourselves, and sometimes they're pretty traumatic. But now you've got the support of each other, you face whatever comes as a two-some, a partnership. You'll find that support and encour-agement a great strength in the years to come.

But you'll also have more burdens than you have ever had before. You'll have the worry of each other's problems as well as your own, the problems of the house, responsi-bilities to the increased number of relatives, and goodness knows what else.

So, to sum it up, on a personal basis your marriage will

challenge you on your deepest levels, and will enable you to reach your highest joys.

I hope that the two sides to your marriage, the public and cosmic, and the personal and private, will each bring you great fulfilment and happiness. I pray that you'll have God's grace and guidance in the years ahead, and that, as you enjoy your own love, you will find his.

As the old gamekeeper said when he made a speech at a wedding, 'May the deer season never end, and the grouse season never begin.'

May God's richest blessing rest upon you both.

34
WEDDING
THE INSTRUCTION BOOK

When you get to open your wedding presents and have a good look at them, there'll be in most boxes an instruction leaflet and a guarantee card. And if you've any sense, you'll read the instructions and fill in the guarantees.

But the greatest gift you have received today is each other as husband and wife. However, there's no guarantee for a happy marriage that comes with it, and no instruction book either! You're on your own, and though God may make a marriage holy, only you can make it good.

After all, you'll be lucky if any of the gadgets you receive and have the instructions for survive for ten years, but your marriage, now that most people live so much longer than they used to, could well last fifty years. Golden wedding anniversaries are very common these days.

So it's worth paying attention to a few instructions, and user-friendly hints. I want to suggest three things that I think would be in that 'Instruction Book for Marriage,' if there was one.

A GOOD MARRIAGE CALLS FOR WORK AND EFFORT

No-one expects to drift into a successful career. If we want to make progress in our job we have to work hard and carefully at it, take on extra courses of study, learn as much as we can about the subject. But marriage? On this subject we expect everything to come dropping into our laps with no effort at all. And of course, it isn't like that — it can't be.

Success in anything, least of all marriage, does not come for free. Great marriages do not drop from heaven ready-made. They come from love freely given, quarrels tolerantly resolved, sacrifices made, and wrongs forgiven. Good marriages, like good art, like good community work, like good anything, have to be worked at.

It's a bit like making a garden. The first clearing of the ground is very labour intensive. But once done you can't leave it, you have to keep clearing the weeds, otherwise it'll go back to wilderness again. Yes, your marriage will need to be worked at.

A GOOD MARRIAGE NEEDS PLENTY OF FORGIVENESS

Spruced up as you are now, you both look splendid, but as you will readily admit, neither of you is actually perfect. And if you don't know that now, you soon will. You will, like everyone else, say things you shouldn't say, do things you shouldn't do, you'll be thoughtless and inconsiderate to each other from day to day, and week to week. Everyone is.

And you have to learn to forgive each other. Not just for the little things, but the big things too. If you don't, you'll drive each other to an intolerable situation. Jesus knew all about forgiveness, of course, and it's worth taking what he said about it seriously. Let it be a full forgiveness. Forgiveness is forgiveness, there's nothing half-way about it. You don't want past mistakes dragged up and thrown at your head every time you put a foot wrong. If your love means anything it means forgiving *and* forgetting.

A GOOD MARRIAGE HAS A SPIRITUAL CONTENT

I don't mean that you have to be regular churchgoers necessarily, though I *do* think that helps, but there should be a respect for all that Christ stood for and was, a secure basis of belief, and moral values in your home. Maintain a respect for standards and virtues that lift you above purely material things, for beauty and truth, for compassion and charity.

Above all, see your love, not as a thing in itself, but as a note in the God of Love's great symphony for the world. In the operation of that love in your home you are harmonizing with the music of the spheres; you are bringing from deep within you something basic about how and why God made the world.

Well, these are just three of the rules from that non-existent 'Instruction Book for Marriage.' There are many others which you'll learn the hard way as you go on.

There's no such thing as the perfect marriage. That would involve perfect people, and there's none of them around. Human nature gets in the way, and you can't have a marriage without human nature. Let's not be naive, but speak of a *good* marriage.

I pray that yours will be good, that it's the kind of relationship in which both of you, conscious of your faults and failings, with all your differences in taste and outlook on life, manage to live together, beautifully, honestly, and happily. I pray, too, that in your marriage you will differ but will not quarrel — hurt each other, but quickly forgive — differ from each other but will be mature enough to see those differences as an enrichment and not a tension.

I hope that as you go on together, hand in hand, you'll tackle each situation as it comes, living life to the full. And then when someone asks out of the blue one day, 'Are you happy?' You'll be able to think, and say, to your own surprise and pleasure, 'Yes, we are!'

May God bless you both.

35
WEDDING
LOVE IS...

Love is the two of you sitting on a lonely bench at Bridlington for two solid hours in February, with the wind straight from Siberia, and not feeling at all cold.

Love is waiting for her at the place you arranged, getting there far too early, and finding that your watch has suddenly decided to slow down to a snail's pace.

Love is being stuck in a day-dream, and finding that whatever you're supposed to be doing, you can't stop thinking of her.

Love is like static electricity when your partner touches you.

Love is having a heated argument about who should give whom the last chocolate biscuit.

Love is a vast telephone bill.

Love is taking enormous trouble over your appearance for his sake, knowing perfectly well that he won't notice.

Love is pretending that you enjoy the sport, when you're really bored to tears.

Love is starting a conversation with your partner, and fifteen minutes later discovering that three hours have gone by.

Love is picking up that roll of wallpaper though it's the one job you can't stand doing.

Love is looking at your wife when her hair is in curlers, and her teeth are in the bathroom — or looking at your husband the morning after the night before, when his eyes are bloodshot and he needs a shave, sighing, and giving them a kiss anyway.

Love is looking at your forty year old partner, but actually *seeing* the attractive young thing that you married.

Love is sharing the same vision, hoping for the same things, being partners in the same pilgrimage.

Love is a child sitting on your lap in tears who says, 'I'm sorry.'

Love is playing 'I Spy', and singing songs with the children on long car journeys.

Love is apologizing quickly for thoughtless remarks and actions, and accepting apologies gracefully.

Love is being willing to let your partner have their own space and times of solitude.

Love is going without something so that you can buy that special present that you know the other really wants.

Love is being ready to let go.

Love is giving your partner a quick kiss when you bump into each other in the shed.

Love is not putting your fingers in your ears when your child starts learning the violin.

Love is never ever rejecting each other, for any reason whatsoever.

Love is the story of Jesus in Matthew, Mark, Luke and John.

Love is often the only atmosphere in which serious problems can be solved.

Love is Christ on the Cross.

Love is always creative, and is the reason why God made the world and us in the first place.

Love is the best word we can use to describe the dynamic which lies underneath the whole of existence.

Love is the way we link in to our world and our destiny.

God is Love.

May God bless you both.

36

FUNERAL

PEACE BE STILL

(on the death of a Christian after a troubled life)

Reading: Mark 4:35-39

We pay tribute today to a lady who was part of our community here in (*name of community*).

(*Details of the years she lived in the place, her upbringing and church connections.*)

And that grounding, not only in character but in the determination to 'go about doing good,' which is so typical of solid Christian upbringing stayed with her all her days. She was part of the world's healing, not its hurt.

(*Details of voluntary work, societies belonged to.*)

Quite apart from all the help she gave to individuals, she followed John Wesley's instruction,

'Do all the Good you can,
In every way you can,
To all the people you can.'

Always friendly and cheerful, she was liked by everyone, which shows that she had mastered the method of giving gracefully. For it isn't only more blessed to give than receive, it's also a lot more difficult to do well.

Of course, this didn't come cheap. No-one knows the

battles she had to fight within herself during the long years of widowhood. Yet she rarely showed it. For this would have shown a weakness she would not have tolerated.

We acknowledge on behalf of all of us in our community, our debt to her over the years.

When Jesus and the disciples were on the lake of Galilee, the usual afternoon wind came blowing down the Valley of the Pigeons and caused a storm on the lake. Jesus said, 'Peace be still,' and as the Bible says, 'The wind dropped and there was a deep calm.'

It's like that in life. As we grow from childhood, to maturity, and old age, we have our storms and frightening moments. We also have our productive times when we get somewhere, and achieve what we want.

At some times in life, God seems to be asleep at the back of the boat, and doesn't seem to be steering, at other times we are so busy — there's so much hustle and bustle — we forget that there's anyone steering at all.

Behind this picture is the assumption that life is a journey — a pilgrimage. That it has a progression, that we have a destination.

That, of course, is the Christian view. Cardinal Hume has pointed out in one of his books that words like 'hope', 'expectation', 'fulfilment' that feature so much in the Church's vocabulary have been stolen by the young, who apply them to this life. They are actually words that should properly be used by the old, because in the nature of things, we look forward to the end of our pilgrimage, to the hope of a life where love dominates, where loving relationships are not handicapped as they are in this world, where love is divorced from the pain that is its inescapable companion in this life.

This was the view of (Deceased). So we rejoice that her pilgrimage has now taken her home, that there she has found so many of her loved ones.

We thank God for her life, and her example, we rejoice that she rowed her oar with the best of them, and pulled her weight through some stormy waters, and that her Saviour has said over her life, 'peace, be still.' And we look forward to the time when we shall reach that calmness, and the relationships broken now will in God's good time be repaired.

We leave her in the safe hands of God, who is more understanding and compassionate than we could ever be, and whose love binds us still, the seen and unseen, in a Kingdom that has no end.

37
FUNERAL

THE INVISIBLE COMFORT
(on the tragic death of a Christian)

My first words must be to you of the family — and clearly they must be words of deep sympathy. Words which I know sum up the feelings of all of us here, and many who can't be here. We have, as far as we have been able, shared the confusion, the uncertainty, the hopes, the fears, and the hurt, you in the family have had to bear during the last weeks.

(*Details of the tragedy or illness, acknowledgement of the efforts, the caring, and the exhaustion of the family, friends, and of any others, such as police, doctors, hospital staff.*)

So many worked so energetically and sensitively. If human activity could have restored her, they would have done it.

For she was a valued member of our fellowship, and of our community, as well as of your family. It is all of us who are grieving today.

But what I think we should remember today isn't these last few weeks, but what she was in her prime — in the many years that you can recall with happiness and satisfaction.

(*Details of her as wife, mother, grandmother, place in the family. Details of jobs, voluntary activities, societies, church connection. Details of her personality, with any suitable anecdotes to sum up her character.*)

Modestly, she would have said she was just an ordinary person trying to live a Christian life. But how we wish there were more like her.

And we'll let the sadness of the last few weeks get lost in a wider celebration of all that she did during a long life.

We pay tribute to a good Christian lady, who is now in a greater glory where human accidents, depressions and ill-nesses have no place.

When Oliver Cromwell lay dying, he was surrounded by a group of weeping friends and relatives. It all got a bit much, so Cromwell said, 'Is there no-one who will praise the Lord?'

So I am sure that she would not have wished us to be miserable today, but to praise the Lord on her behalf. To thank God for a life well-lived, and a course well run.

We thank God for the invisible things, the most basic things, which her life demonstrated.

a. Love is invisible, yet it makes the world go round. It makes life worth living, it provides the warmth, the relationships, the caring that we all need. (Deceased) had that, she expressed it in so many practical ways — and for this we can praise God.

b. Truth is invisible, yet people search for it, fight for it, and are willing to die for it. It's the chance to be true to yourself and live by the best standards you know, and not to live a lie. (Deceased) had that, her beliefs and her actions rang true, they were all of a piece — and for this we can praise God.

c. Personality is invisible, yet we struggle and strain to build our own integrity, and discover what we really are, a special person made in the image of God. And she was that — a real 22 carat personality whom it was a joy to have around — and for that we can praise God.

Those invisible yet very real things are not earthbound qualities. They cannot be measured with a ruler, weighed in a set of scales, or studied under a microscope. They belong to a higher level of living, they have the quality of the eternal about them. Her love and truth and personality have survived death, they endear her now to a greater company than we yet know.

So we bear our sorrow and sadness as we can, but we set it against the picture of a long and good life, which is now in a landscape of God's love and care.

In old cemeteries grave stones often become unreadable. I heard about one very old stone where only the bottom line can now be deciphered. It reads, '. . . gone away with a friend.'

I cannot think of a better epitaph for (*Deceased*). For that friendly soul knew her Lord, and he said that he wanted to call his followers not disciples but friends.

She's now in safe, friendly hands. We know where she is, and we know where we can find her.

38

FUNERAL

DOWN, ROUND, AND UP
(for one without a Christian background)

When I was a young minister just starting out, I asked an old experienced minister what sort of thing I should say at funerals. His answer was a very wise one. 'First you look down, then you look round, then you look up.'

First we look down. We look at the coffin and the flowers, and think of the loved one we've lost. Our minds today are full of memories. Shared experiences with (*Deceased*), joys combined with her, sorrows borne with her. Risks taken jointly, relationships held in spite of all the pressures, generosity given and failures forgiven. Life's like that, especially family life.

And today you pay tribute to one who was part of your life, a sharer in it all, and can be no longer. It's right, and you would want, today, to pay tribute to her for what she was, and the part that she played in all your lives.

No-one can live forever, and what we would all want for ourselves and our loved ones is that, when our time comes, we should be surrounded by the love and care of our relatives and friends; to be remembered fondly and with love.

Bereavement can be selfish, we worry about how all this will affect *us*. So it's a good thing to turn away from ourselves for a moment to think of her, and pray for her. She worried as we all do about death and dying. It's now over for her, the pain has gone, the handicaps dissolved, and I believe her fears have been put to rest. So the first thing we do is take comfort in that thought as we look down, acknowledge all that she meant to us, and say a proper goodbye.

Secondly we look round at ourselves. There will, of course, be a big hole in your lives because of her death. We look around at the family. You will need to knit the broken edges of your relationships together. For the children here, this can be a strange experience. But it's part of what family living is all about, sharing the deepest parts of family life — the birth of babies into the family and the saying goodbye to old people. We share in this way our laughter and our tears. I think it's important that children SHOULD share in these times if they can cope with it. We shut birth and death away into hospitals these days, and shelter our children from what we call the *facts of life*; that's not a healthy thing to do. They need to grasp the realities of family life and its strength at times of crisis.

So you look around at each other, find a solidarity in your shared grief, and even at a time like this, *especially at a time like this*, renew your family commitment to each other.

And lastly, we look up. Figuratively, at least. We look to God, who is behind everything we experience. The more I read and think about the subject of death, the more difficult I find it, and yet, overall, the more simple it becomes. I think the heart of it, and the core of my conclusion, is summed up in the simple text, 'God is Love.'

I believe that there is a purpose in life, and that purpose is personal and loving. That love was expressed in the self-giving of God in Jesus. If that is true, and far better people than me say it is, there are lots of implications.

If God made us for a reason, he is bound to value the highest and best things we know, which are our personalities and our loving relationships.

This means that whatever may be beyond the horizon of life which we call death, we shall survive as *us*, and our loving relationships will be preserved. You can argue about judgement, you can argue about heaven and hell. There are a lot of ideas which people have concerning what happens beyond death that we cannot ever be sure about. I've some of my own, which probably aren't worth tuppence.

But the heart of it is simply 'God is Love.' And he is bound to deal with us in this life and hereafter in a loving way.

That's the most helpful thing I can say to you today. Hold on to 'God is Love,' and I pray that the God, in whose caring hands your loved one is, will be with you all.

I finish with a poem which might help. It's called:

THE ROAD IS SHORT

The loneliness of death is short,
I wasn't on my own for long.
Just like popping out to the shops.
Like saying I'd meet you under the clock.
For soon after I left you, I was met.
Warmly and lovingly met,
By those whose love I'd forgotten,
But they hadn't forgotten me.
Yes, the road was short,
and I had a light to show the way.

The change of death is easy,
For the life of love I've tried to live
is painless here, where God's love is law.
And in this love I am more me
than I have ever been before.
I thank God for your love, and treasure it.
Just as I often prepared the meal
for you to come home to,
think of me preparing to meet you.
In his great love we shall be together again,
Until then, God bless you.

39

GREATHEART IS NOT DEAD
(on the sudden death of a Church stalwart)

Basically, we're all stunned and shocked at what has happened.

(*Details of sudden death, effect on family, friends, community and church.*)

Of course, we want to pass on to (*family names*) our deepest sympathy, in a loss which we all share in a very real way.

Human life is in some ways a very fragile thing — we're at the mercy of a tiny virus, a momentary misjudgement, an inherited weakness. And the events of the past week have reminded us just how frail life is. That frailty of life many times drives us to the faith that is within us. If we know where we've come from, we know why we're here, and know where we're going to. It doesn't prevent our grief, but we can find its proper place.

So today we pay tribute to (*Deceased*), to all that he did and was. Through our tears we can celebrate a life faithfully and generously lived, and a death, if it had to come now, that was within the providence of God.

(*Details of character and personality with anecdotes.*)

We shall miss him dreadfully. People who speak in church, or in the media these days, have to earn their right to be heard. We cannot assume that we shall be listened to out of respect, either for ourselves or the message we have. Perhaps it was so years ago, but not now. These days people look at what we do for our neighbours, for our community, for those who need our help, and if we pass that test *then* they might listen to what we have to say.

(*Deceased*) wasn't a talker, but he was the sort of person who earned *my* right to preach from this pulpit. By countless actions of care and compassion, by generosity in word and deed, by sturdy upright old-fashioned integrity, he created for this church and for his faith such an impression on those who met him, that what's said here began to matter to them.

I remember a conversation he had with me. 'Do you recall a sermon when you asked anyone who'd had a bad week to put their hand up — well I almost did,' said (*Deceased*). 'It had been a week when problems had piled on problems. But then you said, "Who's had a good week?" And I thought, "I've been able to help five people this week." So I reckoned that was a good week, and I put my hand up then.'

That was vintage (*Deceased*) to me. Caring, compassionate, always helping in the background, always thinking of loose ends that ought to be tied up, of things that should be done and dusted. His was a life full of hidden avenues of Christian duty.

But today, we shouldn't only tell ourselves how much we're going to miss him, and what he did, and underline our sadness, but there should be a note of triumph here too.

We celebrate today a steadfast man who won his race faithfully and triumphantly. Who lived a life that was an example to all who follow on. St Paul wrote to the Corinthians, 'Therefore my beloved brethren, be steadfast...' And if anything can sum up (*Deceased*) it's that word — *steadfast*.

It suggests constancy, loyalty to friends, devotion to the family, constancy in his living for the Lord — with strong roots in his home, his community, his church, and his faith. That's (*Deceased*).

The word suggests strength. Integrity of conduct,

honesty of character, facing problems and coping with them. That's (*Deceased*).

It suggests reliability, dependability, thoughtfulness. That's (*Deceased*).

We celebrate today a man who lived an honourable life of Christian steadfastness.

And when we need more of that quality for ourselves, we can still lean upon his memory for it. We shall, in future years, bring him to mind, and by doing so, become more strong, more enduring, and better able to carry life's burdens.

In 1900 the news went round that the great missionary, James Chalmers, had died in New Guinea. He was known as 'Greatheart'. John Oxenham refused to believe he was dead, and wrote this poem.[1]

Greatheart is dead, they say!
Greatheart is dead, they say!
Not dead, not sleeping! he lives on!
His name shall kindle many a heart to equal flame;
The fire he kindled shall burn on and on
Till all darkness in the lands be gone,
And all the kingdoms of the earth be won,
A soul so fiery sweet can never die
But lives, and loves, and works, through all eternity.

Note

1. Quoted in *Chalmers of Papua*, John Oxenham (Carwal Publications, Wallington), 1930.

40

FUNERAL

WHAT WE WOULD WISH

(on the sudden death of an older person)

We are here today to pay tribute to (*Deceased*), to celebrate his life and his achievements, to acknowledge his place in our lives, and to say a respectful and loving goodbye.

As we look at life, and look back on the years that have gone by, as we inevitably do on an occasion like this, there are some suggestions I can make.

What is the best we could hope for — for ourselves and our loved ones?

The first is that we should live long and happy lives. I know it is said that, 'a long life may not be good enough, but a good life is always long enough.' Even so, we'd want for ourselves and those dear to us, long and happy lives.

There is an old Jewish proverb which says that God will judge us by whether we've enjoyed the good things he gave us, or whether we've spurned them. I reckon that's true, and from all I've heard about (*Deceased*), he spent much of his life enjoying the good things that were given to him.

(*Details of length of life, the good things he enjoyed, marriage, family, hobbies, sports, travel.*)

So for (*Deceased*), we can feel that it was a life well lived.

He had his struggles and difficulties as everyone does, but surmounted them with courage and humour. No-one would want an undemanding life that is a bed of roses all the time — that would be so unchallenging as to be monotonous. But we'd want enough hills to climb and sufficient weight to carry, to enable us to develop our strengths, and increase our stature. And that is what happened with (Deceased). We couldn't wish his life to have been any other way, and we look back on his life with happiness. It was long, it was full, it was challenging.

The second thing we would wish for ourselves and our loved ones is that we should be part of the world's healing and not part of its hurt. And that is what you will also remember about (Deceased) By generosity of love and judgement, by genuine concern for others, and by practical help when it was needed, (Deceased) was part of society's answers rather than its questions. He was a plus in our community and not a minus — a giver rather than a taker.

(Details of societies, deeds of helpfulness, general attitude to others.)

Today you will all be remembering fondly, and with a degree of indebtedness, good relationships cemented and good deeds done, and you can recall his life happily.

We would also wish for ourselves and our loved ones that, when our lives end, they should do so peacefully and easily.

And this, too, was the case with (Deceased). Although it all came at the time as a terrific shock, it's what, on thinking about it, we would have wished for him. We would not have wanted, and neither would he, a long and lingering illness.

I'm sure you'd like to pay tribute to all those who did what they could. (Details of those who helped, doctors, ambulance staff, nurses, relatives.)

And lastly, I think we would want for ourselves and our loved ones to be surrounded by the love of our families, the affection of our friends, and the respect of our acquaintances when our time comes.

That indeed is true of (Deceased). The evidence of that is all of us gathered here today to pay tribute to him, all in various degrees filled with memories of him, and all of us having a hole in our lives where (*Deceased*) used to be.

If it is true that none of us can live forever, which it is, then there is nothing evil about lives coming to an end. How can anything so natural, so necessary, and so universal as physical death be anything but the kindly quietus of a loving providence.

As a fruit reaches its full ripeness, so it drops off the tree. If our lives reach three score years and ten, or even longer, and we achieve a ripe old age, we drop naturally into the loving arms of God.

There's no need for Christians to fear death. It's as if we've been to an enjoyable party. We've eaten and drunk lots of nice things. We've met interesting people, and have done our bit to make the party go with a swing for the other guests. And now it's late and we'd like to go home. Would we be afraid to go? Surely not, for we know the home we're going to, we know who is waiting there to meet us, the road is short, and we have a light to show the way.

It's those left behind who are sad. Sad, but not distraught, because we know that sooner or later we shall have to leave, and go home too. And there we shall find him, and many other loved ones.

Some people see death as a great battle to be fought — a mighty river to be crossed against the flood. Perhaps it is for some, but for others, and for (*Deceased*) it has been the gentle translation of a soul from one dimension to a higher. A kindly going home.

We thank God for all that he has been, and is, for us. We leave him in the hands of God, who is always more loving than we could ever be, and ask that his comfort will be with us all.

41

FUNERAL

THE CROSS

(on the accidental death of a young person)

There are no words. No words to sum up what we feel today. Platitudes would inflame rather than soothe our grief. Lofty dogmas are in this context seen to be as remote as, in fact, they always were. Just as a living relationship cannot be described in words, so the loss of it cannot be assuaged by them either.

One moment (Deceased) was one of the lads, the next gone.

One moment (Deceased) had the whole of his life to look forward to, the next no time at all.

One moment, surrounded by family and friends, as shown by all of you gathered here today, the next, separated from us all.

For all of us, particularly those who don't come across death very often it's a devastating blow.

Our technology has failed,

Our love and caring has failed,

Even our language fails.

And we are driven back to our faith — our spiritual resources — that view of life and death we've adopted for our own — and we find out today whether it's a true one, a strong one, or not.

Take away the inhumanity of man to man — and there's plenty of that. Take away the pain we inflict on ourselves — and humankind is remarkably stupid and self-destructive. But take away all of that, and there is still left a core of suffering in this world which is inexplicable, random, accidental, unreasonable — but there.

For it is unreasonable that (*Deceased*) should suffer this. (*Details of upbringing, good contributions made, good aspects of character and personality.*)

While others...

The strength of the Christian faith for me is that it has room for this dark side of life. If Christianity taught that virtue was always followed by health and happiness, and that suffering only came to those who deserved it — I wouldn't believe it. And I certainly wouldn't be standing here telling it to you, because I wouldn't expect you to believe it either.

For it flies in the face of what we see with our own eyes. The world is full of innocent people who are suffering one way or another, all asking the question, 'Why?'

What God did about this deepest and most painful of questions, was not to provide snap and unconvincing answers to it. Neither did he brush aside our human tragedies as beneath his notice.

But he looked at the world with all its injustice and sorrow, and planted a cross in the middle of it — a cross upon which hung all HIS undeserved and unreasonable suffering. He says in effect, 'Your cross is part of my cross, and when it is, you can share in my resurrection.'

Nothing less than a faith like that can fill the hole that (*Deceased*) leaves in our homes and our hearts.

For myself, my sense that behind the tragedy there stands the love of God is greater than my bewilderment at what has happened. There is a God who shares our experiences, sustains us, preserves us, and to whom we shall all be nearer when we die, as we all must.

If that is true, and far greater, wiser and holier people than I say it is, then there will come a time when our relationships, broken now, will be mended, the tears we shed now are dried by laughter, and the pains of grief soothed by love.

And the Cross, seen on noticeboards, placed in churches, hung on gold chains around ladies' necks, will become for us more than just an ornamental symbol, but the sign of a deep consolation, the token of a tremendous hope.

42

FUNERAL

LET THE CHILDREN COME TO ME

(on the death of a child)

My first words must be one of sympathy and condolence to you, especially the family, on this very sad day.

(Details of child, personality, loved place in family. Acknowledge utmost care and love by family, hospital, etc.)

Up to recently in this country, infant mortality was very high and in many parts of the world is even now. People expected that, of the children born to them, only a small number would survive into adulthood. You might have heard old people say of their families that they had so many children, and reared so many of them. Previous generations were used to the thought that death was their constant family companion. The happy years of childhood were set against the background of the fragility of life — epidemics, germs, accident. Death was always in the minds of the Victorians 100 years ago, and in the Third World it still is.

They taught it to the children. A verse of one children's hymn in those days went:

There is an hour when I must die,
Nor do I know how soon t'will come;
A thousand children young as I,

Are called by death to hear their doom.

Nowadays, in the West, we've grown up with the idea that death is something foreign — strange — especially in childhood, and that the medical advances of modern days have abolished it. We regard hospitals as the setting for modern miracles where nothing is impossible.

Of course, it isn't so. We know it isn't — but it still comes as a shock when death shows itself to be part of *our* lives, when it touches *our* family, and we have to try to come to terms with it.

When death visits *our* family and affects *our* relationships we are forced to ask religious questions like, 'Why are we here?', 'Is there any purpose in life?' 'Is there a God, and what is he, she or it, like?' And with the death of a baby or a child, whose life was just a few hours or a few years long, we ask, 'What was it all for?'

These are religious questions, to which I can only give religious answers.

Firstly, God is love, and far more loving to our children than we could ever be. So we need have no fear about (*Deceased*). He is in far better hands than ours, loved by a heart much more caring than ours, and protected by a providence more powerful than ours. Looked at from God's point of view, the problem isn't (*Deceased*), but us. Will this experience bring us nearer to him or not?

Secondly, Christ put great emphasis on children, and loved them. The qualities they possess; their trust, their innocence, their straightforwardness and their love, were close to his heart. 'Let them come to me,' he said, and he blessed them. For children always have many things to teach us adults. In their lives, and sometimes even in their deaths they can say great things, even though they may not be able to string two words together.

Our thoughts are particularly with (*Parents*) at this time. It's a tough time, and you'll have to grapple with this experience between you. It won't be easy.

What matters in life isn't so much what happens, but how to cope with what happens. As you work through your hurt, and ponder over it in your quiet moments, you'll find areas of comfort which help. Cling on to them, develop them.

In particular, grasp hold of the thought that God is Love. You can't get more simple or powerful help than that. He isn't a vague power who doesn't care, but a suffering God who carries our sorrows. And he will never leave you on your own to cope with this by yourselves. He is always there beside you, within you, speaking to you through the tragedy — waiting to comfort and strengthen you.

43

FIGHTING THE GOOD FIGHT
(on the death of an elderly Christian)

Reading: 2 Timothy 4:6-8

St Paul writes to Timothy a second time, and obviously thinks that his life is drawing to a close. He feels what we now call in modern jargon the 'intimations of mortality'. 'I have fought the good fight, I have completed the course, I have kept the faith.'

Paul was a genius as a speaker and writer, and his preaching must have been as prickly as a porcupine with mind-stretching points. Each of these phrases is a welter of significance, especially today as we pay tribute to another one who 'fought the good fight, completed the course, and kept the faith.'

The great Olympic Games in Greece were preceded by a day on which all the athletes met to take a solemn oath. They pledged that they had done not less than ten months' training, that they would not cheat in order to win, and that they would keep their honour as sportsmen.

Paul was saying that, in the great games of life, when all the races had been run, short sprints and long marathons — win some and lose some — he had kept his oath, the promise and commitment was as pure as when he made it, and he remained true to his allegiance to Christ.

Whether (*Deceased*) would say that of himself or not, we can say it for him. You know better than I all the things he did.

(*Details of work done in the church and community.*)

But more than this. Underneath it all, underpinning it all — he was fired and dedicated to the Kingdom this Church represents, and to the Lord it serves. His vision was undimmed, and he kept the values of the faith he proclaimed until the end.

There is an old prayer: 'Lord give me life 'til my work is done, and work 'til my life is ended.' I don't know whether (*Deceased*) ever used that prayer, but whether or no, it was granted. If ever we had cause for a shout of triumph, remembering all that (*Deceased*) did, we should sound it now.

The expression, 'I have kept the faith' also had in Paul's mind a background of business. It was used in his day to mean, 'I have kept the terms of the contract.' Paul had engaged himself to serve his Lord, and he had stood by it, thick and thin. He'd never tried to wheedle out of the spirit of the thing, or go through the fine print to find a 'get-out' clause. He had never let his Lord down, and he kept the faith.

Whether (*Deceased*) would have said that of himself, I don't know. He was probably far too modest. But we can say it for him. Over the years, when difficulties multiplied as they do for all of us — when hope for the future dimmed — when, as happens in life, we go through troughs when nothing seems to go right — in the years when survival seems to come only through hard graft — (*Deceased*) kept his contract with his Lord.

(*Details of any particular problems, e.g. redundancy, illness, family.*)

He was like a rock for others to lean on and rest in the shade of.

So a roll of drums to honour that achievement would not come amiss.

'I have kept the faith' also has the note of optimism in it. It implies that hope is still strong, confidence is still solid, and joy is bubbling under the surface. Certainly that was true of Paul. You and I know that it was also true of (Deceased).

How much joy and hope he had for the young people in his family and in the church. He loved them, and they knew it. In his humour and his enthusiasms he was a character in the nicest sense.

I have a confession to make. When I attend District or Diocesan meetings, as I have to regularly, I look around at all the worthies who gather at such functions — and then I reflect that if I go to heaven I shall be spending eternity with them. Well, I admit that the prospect loses a little of its immediate appeal! But if heaven is liberally spiced with people like (Deceased), who have kept the faith in optimistic joy, and characteristic bubbling good humour, well, I am encouraged to apply for admission.

So for me, if I had an Albert Hall full of people, I'd start them on three cheers for the keeping of a faith like that.

We are sad, of course, but not sorrowful, bereaved but not bitter, grieving but not distraught. How could we be? For someone who generated and was surrounded by so much love while he was with us — for someone who fought the fight so well, completed the course with such honour, and kept the faith so joyfully, how could we be?

Of course, the farther reaches of heaven must lie in paradoxes beyond our human minds, and the profound depths of the love of God must be way beyond our imaginings. But heaven must also start where we are. If God made us as US now, he will remake us as US then. If Jesus died for us as US now, he will love us as US the other side of death.

So we don't have to be heavy-hearted for, as Christians, when we approach the horizon of life that we call death, we do not go into a dark unknown, but into the light of the love of God, recognized and known by the Christ we follow, and surrounded by a cloud of witnesses who loved us before, and love us again.

There's an old funeral prayer which talks about those who make 'the distant heaven a home for our hearts.' Exactly. The only word I quarrel with is the word *distant*. It isn't. It's quite close, and with people like (*Deceased*) there, it's certain to feel like home.

A finer tribute could not be paid than to say he was respected by all who knew him a little, liked by all who knew him better, and loved by those who knew him most.

So, in spite of our tears and sense of loss, we pay tribute today to a Christian gentleman, and with pride we can say of him — he fought the fight, he completed the course, he kept the faith.

44

FUNERAL

I DON'T BELIEVE IN DEATH
(on the death of an elderly person)

I have seen death too often to believe in it. The grim spectres of horrifying nightmares are products of pagan imaginations that know nothing of Easter morning, and are strangers to the love of God.

When I walk through piles of autumn leaves in the park, yellow, russet and red, they're not horrifying — they're beautiful. They are sad in a way, but it won't be long until spring and, if I have the sharp eyes to see them, on some bushes there are even the new buds forming already.

I have sat by dying people too often to think that it's anything but a natural, normal end to an earthly life. Not to all life, but that phase of that life. It's a normal, natural process.

I have attended funerals so often that death isn't a grim stranger, but a familiar friend; as St Francis saw her, 'a kindly Sister Death,' coming to assuage our pain, stop our sufferings, dry our tears, and carry us to a better life.

Dylan Thomas wrote a poem, 'Rage, rage against the dying of the light.' He didn't know what he was talking about. Death isn't the dying of the light, but the coming of it.

I have been with bereaved people too often to kick against the fact of death. With most things we can wriggle and turn — adjust the good, and ameliorate the bad. But with death we're completely helpless — unable to alter anything. This powerlessness makes people illogical, frustrated and angry. Not me, I've seen it often enough to know that there are some things, like love and death, that one just has to accept.

I've thought about death too often to think of it as final. As the Easter story tells us in blinding and confusing detail, it isn't an ending but a withdrawal. It's not a full stop, but a comma. It's like the end of a long journey, when the driver stops the engine, turns off the lights, opens the car door, gets out of the car, and walks up the path to the home that lies waiting.

So it's against this background that I pass on to you my sympathy on the death of (Deceased), a background that gives hope and real comfort, as we pay tribute to her life.

(*Details of person, career, hobbies, family, character and personality.*)

It would be possible today, I suppose, for me to use well-worn religious language thoughtlessly, and say the expected traditional things, so that they could wash over you to comfort the hurt that you feel. But this wouldn't be right. I offer you the only real comfort that I know.

Human death is part of the providence of God — part of his great design, and must come to us all. There is nothing unusual or evil about it. The other thing is the love of God — never under-estimate that factor. For if he loves us when we are distracted from him by all our concerns and cares in this world, how much more will he love us when we are nearer him in the next.

Benjamin Franklin wrote on the death of his brother:

A man isn't completely born until he is dead. Why then should we grieve...We are spirits. That bodies should be lent us, while they can afford us pleasure, assist us in acquiring knowledge or in doing good to our fellow creatures, is a kind and benevolent act of God. When they become unfit for these purposes and afford us pain instead of pleasure, instead of an aid become an encumbrance, it is equally kind and benevolent that a way is provided by which we may get rid of them. Death is that way. Our friend and we were invited abroad on a party of pleasure which is to last forever. His chair was ready first and he is gone before us. We could not all conveniently start together; so why should you and I be grieved at this, since we so soon to follow and know where to find him?

45

FUNERAL

THE VICTIM
(on the death of a suicide)

My first words must be those of sympathy for you, the family and friends of (*Deceased*). The experience of the last few weeks, culminating in this service today — is something you would not wish to go through again. It's been a very sad time, and your memories will be sad ones.

(*Details of person, brief life story, last weeks.*)

There was a tombstone I read about which had on it the very human words, 'I expected this — but not yet.' And that's a feeling we all share today.

Life's a mixture of ups and downs — good days and bad — good years and bad. Sometimes we live life, and sometimes it lives us. On occasion we are in command, at other times our diaries and bank accounts dictate to us what we can and can't do. In some circumstances we are the victors, and at others we are the victims.

This was true in (*Deceased's*) case. But in his case he was far more often the victim, vanquished by powers he could not fight, by influences he could not resist. None of us know all the battles he fought, and all the defeats he suffered.

To me, the great strength of the Christian faith is that it

has something to say to us whatever our condition when life has finished with us.

When we are victors, and things have gone well, the message is of duties and responsibilities, especially to the weak and defenceless. We shall be judged, so Jesus said, by how we fed the hungry, sheltered the homeless, comforted the afflicted. However strong you may feel, implies the New Testament, you still depend on God — on his ever-sustaining life flowing through you. You are not a separate 'self-made person', but are still answerable to him.

And that's a salutary reminder to us when life goes smoothly, when we get a bit too big for our boots, and tragedies are things that happen to other people.

But at times when we are the victim, when we are beaten down and defeated, the Christian faith still speaks to us. Because we see Jesus Christ as the victim in the great event of Good Friday. He, too, suffered unjustly. He, too, was the victim of forces outside himself, negative, destructive forces, which in the end killed him.

He took our victimization upon himself, and he knew what it felt like. We see in the Gospel records of what happened and Jesus' reactions to suffering. They were of forgiveness, acceptance and concern. For most of us, suffering makes us preoccupied and selfish — not in Jesus' case — that's what was so startling. I'm sure that now that (*Deceased*) is in His nearer presence, that forgiveness, acceptance and concern will be showed to him as well. (*Deceased*) will be receiving now in God's love, qualities that he rarely saw in his troubled life.

So I find even in the sad events of today, a hope and a comfort in my Christian faith. For life and death, are either religious or absurd. They either have some sort of background meaning or life and its conclusion are, in Shakespeare's words, 'a tale told by idiots.' But looked at from the perspective of the Christian, the riddles of sorrow and death, the mysteries of victors and victims, can find a meaning. I know of nothing else that can put any kind of honest perspective on it, and bring us comfort.

It brings us strength and help when we, as we all must,

reach the end of our earthly lives, and launch into the great sunlit uplands of the love of God. May that love be with us all.

46

FUNERAL

THE JOURNEY

(on the death of an elderly person)

Today, we celebrate someone who lived a long and satisfying life. We recognize that her body had broken down; her quality of life was far less than she would have wanted, or that we would wish for her. She'd seen enough, experienced enough, of life's joys and sorrows. And many of her loved ones had gone before; she was one of the last of her generation.

So it's not in any sense of great sorrow that we pay tribute to her today. Her bag was packed — she was mentally and spiritually prepared, ready to go. So as well as the natural sadness we must all feel, there is, mingled with it, a feeling of fulfilment, completion, and conclusion, about this service.

First we pay tribute, as we should today, to what she was and did. We remember what she was in her prime.

(*Details of life, character, achievements.*)

There is an old, rather silly story, about an old lady who died. Her daughter had a five year old girl. So she took her on her knee and said, 'Grandma's gone away.' 'Where to?' asked the little girl. 'To heaven,' said the mother, expecting the little girl to be very upset. But she wasn't. Her reaction was, 'Oh, that's all right then, Grandpa's sure to be at the station to meet her.'

There's more to this story than meets the eye, because death and bereavement are very much like that.

When we have visitors, welcome friends or relatives, and the time comes for them to go home, the hours just before they go are always a bit sad and tense, aren't they. The business of saying, 'goodbye', casts a shadow before it, and nobody likes it.

Just in that way, when someone like (*Deceased*) dies, there is this tense and uncomfortable last few days or hours. One does one's best, and I'm sure that you did yours, but we're never quite sure of ourselves.

Then, if you go down to the station to see them off, they get on the train, and we are left standing on the platform. We're separated — we can see each other, but we can't talk through the double glazing, the odd rough gesture is all we can do. And when someone dies, gradually fading away, as (*Deceased*) did, we're in that position too, for the last little while. We can hold their hand, let them know we're there, but communication has faded away. There's nothing we can say. Just *be* there.

Then the train leaves, it gets smaller, disappears into the distance, and after a last wave, they have gone. Disappeared. Like when this service finishes, and you go home, she will have gone. There will be plenty of evidence that she has been, things to sort out and tidy, happy memories to recall, but (*Deceased*) as a person has gone.

There is one other similarity. To her, on the train, she has not got any less. She has not been diminished in any way. To her, the excitement is who is waiting for her at the other end of the journey. She will be looking forward to being lovingly met, warmly greeted, and affectionately welcomed. 'Grandpa's sure to be at the station to meet her.'

Life is a journey, a pilgrimage, a voyage of discovery. It's a series of irreplaceable and unrepeatable experiences which carry us to whatever personal development we can reach. And all the evidence I can find seems to show clearly that death is not the end of the journey, but a staging post to a greater future.

Werner von Braun, the German rocket scientist, said once,

Science tells us that nothing in nature, even the tiniest particle, can disappear without trace. Nature does not know extinction — all it knows is transformation. Everything science has taught me strengthens my belief in the continuity of our spiritual existence after death. Nothing disappears without trace.

Add to this the teaching of Jesus Christ about a God of Love, who loves us as people whatever we've done, and whose kingdom spans life here and life hereafter. In addition, add a kingdom where the language is love, the time is measured in joyful moments, and the currency is peace.

Then, when we think of (Deceased), we can be thankful for all that she meant to us — we can feel a fitting sense of the finale about today, and can go home with the peace of God in our hearts.

47

FUNERAL

THE TRUMPET SHALL SOUND
(at the end of a long Christian life)

An English statesman was in Westminster Abbey, attending the funeral of Robert Browning, the poet. He was depressed by the solemn gloom of the whole service. Afterwards he said, 'I would have given something for a banner or two, and much would I have given if a chorister had come out and rent the air with a trumpet.'

And so would we all, at a time like this. The trumpets of triumph should sound when a good man dies, full of years, filled with faith, and surrounded by so much love and affection as (*Deceased*) is today.

When Christian in *Pilgrim's Progress* crossed that last river, the trumpets sounded for him on the other shore. And when a true Christian approaches immortality, it should be the fanfare of victory that rings in our ears, not the melancholy dirge of defeat.

First, there should be a fanfare for the Christ who rose from the dead on that first Easter Sunday, and whose new life all Christians share. He rose, not for himself alone, but so that we who live in him, should live on with him.

So we have no hesitation about our loved one. (*Deceased*) lived his life to the full. He travelled a great deal, met all sorts of people; he saw them at their best and at their worst.

But he didn't allow this to make him cynical; rather, he remained the warm, outgoing and straight man he always was. That he was upright and honourable to the end is something you in the family can remember with pride, and all of us can regard as a victory.

His was not a faith which he wore on his sleeve, but kept it burning brightly in his heart, and expressed in all the dealings of his daily life.

Here was a Christian gentleman who never let us or anybody down, he never let Jesus down either. And he did it, not with cold, grim righteousness, but with the humour and smiles that only come from one with a loving heart, and one at peace with himself. He lived in happy friendship with his Lord, and shared his resurrection life.

Praise God for that. It's worth a good fanfare.

Then let's give the trumpet another blow because death isn't an end but a beginning — not destruction but a transformation. All the indications we have from our faith is that it is for all faithful souls, a glorious fulfilment.

For those who love God, heaven means being closer to his love; for those who try to love their neighbours, heaven also means being closer to them. And (Deceased) knew how to love both, and did. So for him, the trumpets are indeed sounding on the other side. Think of how many relationships have been mended by his passing, and those relationships broken now will all too soon be repaired.

The Church is the one organisation in this world which never loses a member by death. They're promoted to the Church Triumphant. They join the majority, that assembly of wise and wonderfully loving people, whose names we only dimly remember, or whom we only read about. (Deceased) is now among them, and a great time he must be having.

That's a mighty good reason for a second fanfare.

Let us blow a third fanfare because the death of a Christian isn't a disaster, it's arriving at a destination. It's getting safely home after a dangerous and problematic journey. It's being greeted warmly, being congratulated by loved ones who've been waiting anxiously for us.

All down the ages there have been Christians who've had more curiosity than sense, who have made all sorts of weird speculations about what the life after death is like. And mighty queer most of those guesses have been. Let's be honest, we don't know! I don't think wild guesses, or pictures of thrones and pearly gates get us anywhere. The important thing, surely, is who is there.

If a man had a dog, and tied him to the railings before going into a house, the dog wouldn't want to know what the furniture in the house is like, how many rooms it has, or the colour of the wallpaper. All he knows is that his master is in there, and that's why he wants to get in.

Why should we worry about the unimportant details of eternal life? Why bother about what the furniture of heaven is like? All we need to know is that our master is there, and with him all those loving people, including (*Deceased*) who have gone before.

If indeed, 'nothing can separate us from the love of God in Jesus — neither death nor life,' then we can praise God for it, and leave our loved ones in the security of that love.

And if a faith like that isn't worth a third fanfare of trumpets, I don't know what is!

You in the family will miss him greatly. There will be a great gap in the family circle which you can only fill by holding each other more closely. Yes, our community will miss him. We can ill afford to lose men of the quality of (*Deceased*). And there will for all of us be moments when we feel the loss very much.

But at those moments, we shall at the same time hear the distant echo of triumph for a man who lived life well, and departed from us respected, honoured and loved. And for whom 'the trumpets sounded, and the dead were raised, incorruptible.'

48

FUNERAL

FITTING INTO HEAVEN
(on the death of a gracious lady)

We celebrate today the life of (*Deceased*). We pay tribute to a person whose enjoyed a full life, who put more than her due into the relationships which she had, who could look back on life with a sense of satisfaction, and not with regret.

(*Details of life story, anecdotes and character.*)

When we reach the bump in our pilgrimage road, that horizon beyond which we cannot see anything but blue sky, that interruption in our view that we call death — what is there over the hill?

There have been all sorts of pictures drawn, speculations about heaven and hell that are very human, and many of them, I guess, must be very wrong. I don't think it's worth spending time on them, all I am sure of is that when we get there we are nearer God's love. This is a love that is creative, because God made us, and self-giving because he sent Jesus to redeem us.

Perhaps heaven and hell are not places at all, but just being near to God and our neighbour. If we love him and them — that will be heaven; if we don't — that will be hell.

George Matheson, that blind Scottish Presbyterian minister of the last century, said, 'Save me, O Father, from an uncongenial heaven!' And how true that cry from the heart is.

We need have no fear about whether God will receive us. Like the forgiving father in the Prodigal Son story, he will run to welcome us, and kill the fatted calf for us. We need have no fear that we shall be driven from God's presence — rejected by his love.

No, the problem we have is whether we shall be able to respond to it. Will we stand by the Jordan river and have no eye for its beauty? Will we walk along the green pastures and be colour-blind? Will we listen to the heavenly choir and be tone deaf? Will we be enrolled in the body of heavenly Samaritans and have no heart for their kindness? Or stand among the saved without knowing our Saviour? Find me a better definition of hell!

May God grant that, when we reach that Kingdom where the currency is love, joy, and peace, we shall not arrive bankrupt.

In (*Deceased's*) case, we can rest assured that she has fitted in as well there as she did among us. That friendly and loving soul has found her home with others of like mind. (*Deceased's*) capacity to love which she showed in the years she was with us, in the family, among her friends, and to the community here, grew from year to year. This wealth of love fitted her for the life she now lives.

She had one rare and precious gift, which not everyone possesses. She could receive gracefully. As Christian people, we are so used to giving and serving others. We are commanded to by Jesus, and we take that commission very seriously. We teach our children to do it, and try to give them good role models. But the time comes, mostly at the end of life, when we cannot contribute any longer, and we have to be on the receiving end. It's a vital role, because for every giver there has to be a receiver. It's a difficult thing to do well, because we don't like to feel beholden to anyone, or that we're imposing ourselves on others. Perhaps it's just as well that this is left to the end of our lives when we're a bit older and wiser. To be able to welcome a neighbour's visit and send them away happier than when they came; to accept a parcel from a young Brownie and make her feel good about having delivered it; to give a friendly wave to the paper boy and make it the highlight of his round; it is a hard thing to do well, and some people never learn how.

But (*Deceased*) did. She had learned the art of receiving graciously, and, although she wouldn't have recognized it, probably did as much good in her last infirm years, than she did when she was young and active.

And because of that, and the sort of person she was and is, we need have no fears about her happiness now. For heaven, whatever it is like, is full of giving and receiving, of the love, joy and peace, which (*Deceased*) showed in her daily life among us.

She is in harmony with the God of Love whom she served in the past, and now serves in a greater light. She now receives greater mercies from her maker than she ever saw in this life, and I'm sure does so as graciously. May that God give comfort to us today, and encourage us to follow her example.